CW01023923

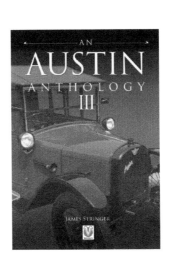

www.veloce.co.uk

First published in August 2023 by Veloce Publishing Limited, Veloce House, Parkway Farm Business Park, Middle Farm Way, Poundbury, Dorchester DT1 3AR, England.
Tel +44 (0)1305 260068 / Fax 01305 250479 / e-mail info@veloce.co.uk / web www.veloce.co.uk and www.velocebooks.com.
ISBN: 978-1-787116-50-4; UPC: 6-36847-01650-0.
© 2023 James Stringer and Veloce Publishing. All rights reserved. With the exception of quoting brief passages for the purpose of review, no part of this publication may be recorded, reproduced or transmitted by any means, including photocopying, without the written permission of Veloce Publishing Ltd. Throughout this book logos, model names and designations, etc, have been used for the purposes of identification, illustration and decoration. Such names are the property of the trademark holder as this is not an official publication. Readers with ideas for automotive books, or books on other transport or related hobby subjects, are invited to write to the editorial director of Veloce Publishing at the above address. British Library Cataloguing in Publication Data – A catalogue record for this book is available from the British Library. Typesetting, design and page make-up all by Veloce Publishing Ltd on Apple Mac. Printed by TJ Books, Padstow, Cornwall, UK.

AN
AUSTIN
ANTHOLOGY
III

JAMES STRINGER

VELOCE

CONTENTS

Dedication

I dedicate this book to the memory of the late Robert John (Bob) Wyatt MBE, who, back in 1958, encouraged owners of vintage Austin Twelves to come together in a bid to ensure that these sturdy, well-designed motor cars would still be around for many years to come.

After writing three books on the Company's history and its products, Bob had established himself as the undisputed authority on all matters Austin.

When I told him that it was my intention to write a book covering many of the lesser known aspects of the Austin, its products, and the people who manufactured or owned them – stories that had never been fully covered before – he could not have been more supportive, and encouraged me to go ahead: he even offered to provide the Foreword to the first book, which, of course, I gratefully accepted.

So, in dedicating *An Austin Anthology III* to Bob, I do so in the knowledge that without his help and guidance, these stories may never have been fully researched or told.

Foreword

The arrival in my mailbox of Jim Stringer's second *Austin Anthology* coincided with an invitation from my old friend to pen a brief welcome to his third, then in the final stages of preparation. It was a pleasure, and a privilege, to accept.

Back in the early 1960s, when in the first flush of our mutual fascination with ancient Austins, Jim and I could have had no notion that, more than fifty years on, we would still be in love with the grand old brand, and doing our bit for the cause.

Jim's 'bit' has turned out to be rather more of an affair. During his many years of sterling service for the Vintage Austin Register, he formed a valuable relationship with Austin family members, one-time Company employees and associates and, by dint of some Holmesian detective work, built up the marvellous collection of anecdotes, photographs and memorabilia from which his anthologies have been drawn.

Whilst some of Jim's tales have appeared in print before, others are new, and what a joy it is to find them all finely tuned, neatly bound and preserved together for posterity.

Whether you've a well-developed sense of history or just like to dabble in nostalgia and intrigue, Jim's first two volumes are sure to have tickled your fancy, and I am certain that *Anthology III* will do likewise.

Among its many tempting titbits are the Company's receivership crisis of 1921 and, just a few years later, a narrowly-averted takeover bid from General Motors. Also on offer is the tale of a fascinating but failed French connection; the story of the village Sir Herbert created for his loyal employees, and, from as recently as the early 1960s, the adventures of 'Mugwump,' a 1930 Austin 16/6 that was driven by university students from Bristol to Cape Town and then back again.

This should be plenty to pique your interest, but the quintessence of any story lies, above all, in the telling. I feel sure that, on the evidence thus far, Jim Stringer has amply demonstrated his expertise in this department, and that what you are about to read will whet your appetite for even more.

Peter Fry
(Patron of the New Zealand
Vintage Austin Register)

Introduction

About the author

I was born in the West London suburb of Shepherd's Bush in January 1943, during the time when the Luftwaffe was busy carrying out a bombing raid on the capital. Brought home from the hospital a week or so later through the debris-strewn streets in the comfort and safety of a 1935 Austin Taxicab with coachwork by Jones Bros' of Westbourne Grove, thus commenced an instant affection for all things 'Austin.' The taxicab was owned Mr Brewer, an elderly neighbour who sported an intriguing waxed moustache!

When old enough to drive I purchased a 1929 Austin 16/6 with rare Fabric Saloon coachwork, much to my father's dismay. The relationship was not improved upon when, despite being told not to put the car in the garage where we lived, I defied my father, as teenagers often do, and almost destroyed the doors at the far end of it when putting the car away for the first time, after having pressed the accelerator pedal instead of the one that should have stopped it! That same Austin still holds pride of place in the Stringer household to this day.

On purchasing the Austin for the princely sum of £35, I then became a member of the Vintage Austin Register, and very soon became involved in its running, from initially helping with the first newsletter, to becoming the Hon Sec, then Chairman. I then 'retired,' but two years later took on the job of producing the Register's glossy quarterly

magazine as its editor. Not content with waiting for contributions to be sent in by its members, I started to undertake research into many stories concerning Austin vehicles, aeroplanes, and, of course, the people who purchased them, drove them, flew them, or were just simply involved in their manufacture – stories that, up until now, had not been thoroughly documented. It is these that form the basis of this, my third anthology.

About the book

When I decided to commit to paper the various stories associated with Austin, it was not necessarily my intention to write a comprehensive history of the Company as such, but to focus upon some of the products and people that may not have been fully researched or written about before. Hence the story of 'Pobble' the 1906 40hp racing car, the Austin 'Whippet' bi-plane and Harry Austin, Herbert's much loved younger brother all of which I covered in my first Anthology.

An Austin Anthology attracted many favourable comments, which encouraged me to write a second book along much the same lines, published in early 2019.

Within the pages of *An Austin Anthology* and *An Austin Anthology II* I provided the reader with a wider understanding of the important role The Austin Motor Company played in the development of the motor car, and how, through the engineering skills of Herbert Austin and his team of designers, engineers and craftsmen, he was able to manufacture motor cars that were not only 'right' at the time but which have since stood the test of time by outliving many of their contemporaries, as can be seen by their remarkable survival rate.

In this third book, I have taken what I believe to be a final trawl of stories associated in one way or another with Austin, and brought them to life under one cover. My research has been kindly supported by many individuals who have helped or advised me, to ensure total accuracy of the stories within. I have also made good use of early editions of the *Austin Magazine* and its predecessor *The Austin Advocate Magazine*, the latter dating back to 1911, which in themselves provide the historian with a wealth of information and illustrations.

The stories within tell how the iconic Austin 'Wings & Wheel' logo came about, and how the last of the luxurious Sizaire Berwick motor cars were actually Austin Twelves and Twenties in disguise. You will find out about a couple of Cambridge University student pranks that led to Austin Sevens being 'parked' in the most inappropriate places, and how another group of students, this time from Bristol University, drove a 32-year-old Austin 16/6 down through Europe and Africa to Cape Town, and the car was then driven back to Bristol by four students from Cape Town University. There is also the story behind the 1930 Austin 12/4 that was owned by Spike Milligan and sold on to Peter Sellers, and you can read about the time when the Company fell upon hard times and was put into the hands of the receiver: a move that almost resulted in the Company being taken over by General Motors of America, but was then saved by a simple toss of a coin.

In conducting research, and recording these stories for posterity, I hope to have provided the reader with an enjoyable insight into Herbert Austin's motor car company, and the products that he produced, many thousands of which are still providing pleasurable motoring for their owners to this day.

James (Jim) Stringer

Acknowledgements

I am indebted to Gray-Adams for its generosity in sponsoring *An Austin Anthology III*, without which the book may never have been published.

DESIGNERS & MANUFACTURERS OF
QUALITY REFRIGERATED & DRY FREIGHT VEHICLES
FRASERBURGH

My thanks are also extended to the Austin Ex-Apprentices Association and to Mr Ivor Vaughan (an Austin ex-apprentice) for their contribution towards the book's publication.

In compiling this work, which covers a few of the lesser known activities of the Austin Motor Company, its products and those who had experience with them, it was sometimes necessary to consult the works of others who have previously touched upon the same subjects. Where the authors of such research are known, their work in this respect is gratefully acknowledged.

Thanks go to the late Val Biro for photographs and information on Gumdrop; the Longbridge Village Preservation group for help with the Austin Village story; Mike Worthington – Williams, Martyn Nutland and *Motor Sport* for help and illustrations for Sizaire Berwick; the late Bob Wyatt for the wings and wheel story; Robert Crawley for information regarding the Sidmouth toast-racks; Anthony Mealing for the story on the Austin 8 left behind at Dunkirk; John Baker (Austin Memories.com), who, amongst other things provided information and illustrations supporting the Austin tractor story. I would also mention the late Gerald Walker for his detailed account of the Cambridge University pranks, and Tom Johnson for the photograph of the Austin Seven suspended under the bridge; Roger Freshman who, with Victor Szechenyi, Andrew Quick, Patrick Collins of the National Motor Museum, Beaulieu, and Hugh Amoore from the *Cape*

Argus, provided details and photographs for the story of Mugwump; Richard Williams and Allan Dyer for the story and photographs of the 12/4 owned by Peter Sellers; and Jack Peppiatt for the story of his journey from Buenos Aires to New York in three Austin Sevens.

Mention should also be made of the assistance given by members of the Brough Superior Motorcycle club for their input into the story of the BS4, and Dr E Molem for providing details and assistance with the story concerning the early Austin publicity illustrations, with additional information provided by the Austin Seven Club's Association archivist, Phil Baildon. Finally, Barry Quann of BMC World, who kindly supplied stills from *The Mighty Atom*.

Author's Note
The author would like to apologise for the quality of several of the photographs and images used within the text of this book. This is mainly due to the age of the images and the sources from which they were obtained.

Chapter 1

An Austin named Gumdrop

Balint Stephen Biro was born on 6th October 1921 in the Hungarian capital of Budapest, where he and his older sister grew up in a large flat overlooking the Hungarian Parliament building. His father practiced law and his mother was a socialite who, in the 1920s and '30s, took an active part in Budapest society.

Val Biro and Gumdrop. (Courtesy Mike Hodgson)

The young Balint was educated at the Cistercian School in Budapest, and later went on to study at the Jaschnik School of Art.

In 1939, concerned about the rise of Adolf Hitler and the uncertain future that may lie ahead, Balint's father made the decision to send him to England, where he was enrolled at the Central School of Art in London to study illustration and wood engraving. As the war progressed the school was evacuated to the Midlands, where Balint was able to continue with his studies in comparative safety.

With that decision, Balint's father probably saved his life as, within a couple of years, Germany had seized control of Hungary, and it then became part of Hitler's Axis force.

The status of being registered as a student saved young Balint from being interned by the British as an 'enemy of the state,' and he was therefore allowed to continue with his studies. On graduating in 1942 he attempted to enlist for active service, but was limited to driving an ambulance or working for the fire brigade, and it was the latter that he decided upon.

In late 1944, the tide began to turn against Germany, and its forces were by then stretched to the limit on several fronts. But Joseph Stalin had in mind to take over Hungary and add it to his now growing Soviet Union. There then ensued a battle that put Budapest and the occupying German Army under siege, as the advancing Russian Army had now totally surrounded the city, followed by relentless bombing from the air and shelling from ground troops. The conflict finally ended in the early months of 1945, leaving the once-beautiful and historic city of Budapest almost totally destroyed by Soviet forces.

With his former home and almost a third of Budapest destroyed, there was little reason for Balint to return to his native Hungary once the war was over, so he took the decision to apply for British citizenship, change his Christian name to Val and settle down to start a new life in England.

With Val's amazing skill as an illustrator, he found it very easy to obtain commissions for his work, and designed book covers for authors such as Neville Shute, Nigel Tranter, and CS Forester, and even covers for the *Radio Times*.

By the late 1940s Val had married and moved to the Buckinghamshire town of Amersham, where he purchased his very first motor car. As his wife's family had always had Austins it was only natural that their first car should also be that make, and so in 1950 they purchased a 1933 Austin Seven. When Val's wife first saw the car she noted that the first two letters of the registration plate were 'G' and 'M,' and immediately christened it 'GUMDROP.' This car was eventually replaced by another Austin, a 1938 8hp open tourer, which, sadly, did not live up to the reputation of being 'dependable' and so was soon disposed of.

Their next car was a brand new Austin A40 Somerset saloon that they named Matilda, which, like the 8hp, was not a very satisfactory vehicle: after incurring several hefty repair bills, Matilda was also disposed of.

The Biros now relied upon a different type of 'horse power' in the shape of an 1880 Brougham drawn by a bay mare named Cherry. Whilst this was ideal for local trips, the need to undertake longer journeys – together with the fact that Cherry was getting on in years – meant that the Brougham was eventually sold, and replaced by a 1926 Austin 12/4 Clifton Tourer.

Val had not set out to purchase the Clifton, but came across it whilst on his way to view – and probably purchase – a 1948 Rover 8 that he had been told about. However, as he stopped for fuel at an old-fashioned garage in the village of Hardwick, he spotted a very old car parked at the rear of several others being offered for sale.

On enquiring about this particular motor car, Val was informed it was being sold on behalf of the local scrap dealer, who considered it too good to scrap, so had 'done it up' to make it presentable to sell on, although Val was advised that the engine might require money to be spent on it as it was 'on its last legs.' So, in 1961, and for just £100, Val became the proud owner of a 1926 Austin 12/4 Clifton Tourer that his wife immediately named Gumdrop, because, after all, it was an Austin and just a little larger than their original Gumdrop, the 1933 Austin Seven.

Once home, and with the engine attended to, Gumdrop was to make several major journeys to Scotland and Cornwall, and was considered so reliable that it was used as Val's normal everyday means of transport.

A couple of years after buying Gumdrop, Val received a commission for a book illustration from Mr Ewart Wharmby of Brockhampton Press, 75 miles away in Leicester. Val drove there in Gumdrop to discuss what was required, and over lunch the pair not only discussed the commission, but Val told Ewart all about his Austin 12/4. Back at the office, once the business side of their meeting was concluded, and just as Val was about to leave, Ewart called him back and asked if he had ever thought about writing a book about the car he was so passionate about, and that, if he were to do so, Ewart would love to see it.

On the journey back to Amersham Val was occupied by many thoughts circulating around his head about how best to approach the idea put there by Ewart. A children's book, yes, featuring Gumdrop, but would it ever be published?

On arriving home, his thoughts throughout the return journey were put down on paper, revised and rewritten, and finally typed out, and within just two days of his returning from Leicester, *Gumdrop: The Adventures of a Vintage Car* had been written.

In 1967, a year after the book was published, Ewart suggested that another book featuring Gumdrop could be worth considering, as the first one had been received very well. This turned out to be *Gumdrop and the Farmer's Friend*, which featured a 1903 Fowler Traction Engine and a 1905 De Dion-Bouton, both actual vehicles owned by friends of Val.

This book attracted the attention of the BBC, which thought it would be rather a good idea to adapt it for the children's television programme *Play School,* using the actual vehicles featured in the story. The success of this led to other television appearances on both the BBC and ITV.

Gumdrop – The Adventures of a Vintage Car: Val Biro's first book featuring his 1926 Austin 12/4 Clifton Tourer. (Courtesy the late Val Biro)

On one such programme, Val was to drive Gumdrop into the studio, but because of health and safety issues, the petrol tank had to be drained before it could be allowed in. With an empty tank and the cameras rolling, Gumdrop was gently pushed into shot, the sound of its engine dubbed in.

Gumdrop and The Farmer's Friend – on location. (Courtesy the late Val Biro)

On another occasion, but this time for ITV's Thames Television, the late Sir (later Lord) Bernard Miles, was to read one of the Gumdrop stories, but during the dummy run it became obvious that he was not comfortable with this. After a break for lunch, he returned all smiles, however, declaring that he had now found the 'right voice' to fit the story. The subsequent reading was, of course, perfect.

In a later book, *Gumdrop on the Brighton Run* (1976), launched on the first Sunday in November when the London to Brighton Run was held, Val was given permission by the RAC – organiser of the event – for Gumdrop to be parked on Madeira Drive with the arriving Veteran cars. It should be noted that, in the story, Gumdrop had been given the title "An Honorary Veteran Extraordinary."

Val with Sir (later Lord) Bernard Miles.
(Courtesy the late Val Biro)

Gumdrop on Madeira Drive, ready to welcome
competitors of the London to Brighton Run.
(Courtesy the late Val Biro)

By now the Gumdrop books had become established as easy reading for children, and encouraged those who had never previously read a book to pick up a Gumdrop book as their first approach. Val also agreed to take Gumdrop to a local primary school to read one of his stories to the children. This, of course, led to Gumdrop being driven further and further afield to satisfy requests for public appearances, totting up an average of over 6000 miles every year.

On one such trip to the Yorkshire village of Ilkley, Val was asked to park Gumdrop alongside a very long wall that had recently been given a coat of white paint. Val was handed brushes and tins of household paint, and asked to paint a mural on the wall. Following an outline in chalk, Val handed the paint and brushes to the children and supervised their efforts on the Gumdrop mural, which they painted to good effect. I wonder if that mural still exists ...?

A frequently asked question when visiting schools was how Gumdrop got its name? Considering that the real reason might seem a little dull, Val made up a fictitious story, later included in *Gumdrop Makes a Start*, which involved a small boy watching the new cars coming through the gates of the Austin Factory in 1926.

Gumdrop and the Ilkley mural.
(Courtesy the late Val Biro)

"As he stood watching, he saw a slightly different car being rolled onto the forecourt. He opened his eyes even wider than usual, because somehow this car was different. It was blue with black wings and a brass radiator. It had a black hood and four brass lamps that sparkled in the sunshine, but what made this car different was the curly brass horn bolted to the windscreen! This was the most beautiful Austin Clifton heavy 12 that he had ever seen in his life."

Val then went on to describe the business of starting it on the button, and the car first makes a 'gummmm' noise and then a sort of 'drropopopop' sound. The boy was enchanted.

"As if the car had called out its own name. 'That's it' he declared to one and all, 'That's his name, GUMDROP.' The boy felt convinced that Gumdrop was the only car for him, and he longed to have that beautiful car for his very own. As he was just seven years old, however, there was little hope of that. Taking a last lingering look he walked home in a dream."

It wasn't until 34 years later that the boy (Josiah Oldcastle), now grown up, discovered the car in a scrap yard, which, of course, he promptly buys.

Mr Josiah Oldcastle, the first owner of Gumdrop in the story books.
(Courtesy the late Val Biro)

The story continued: "He was beside himself with joy, and could hardly stop himself from dancing around as he pumped up the tyres. Settling in the driving seat he marvelled that his dream had come true and Gumdrop was his at last."

Josiah Oldcastle, with his faithful dog, Horace, were regular characters in many of the Gumdrop adventures.

In June 2010 I contacted the production manager of the Oxford Diecast Limited to suggest that a 1/43 scale model of a 1926 Austin Clifton tourer would make an excellent addition to its range of model cars. To endorse my case I also sent a picture of Gumdrop and a copy of the front cover of *Gumdrop's Merry Christmas*. The following June I was advised that ODL was about to go ahead with my suggestion, and requested Val's contact details. Val, of course, knew nothing of this, and was thrilled to bits when I told him. He later told me that ODL had called to see him and Gumdrop, and had taken hundreds of photographs and measurements of the car during the visit. It was just over a year later, in July 2012, that the model was released as AHT001, to be followed by

The Oxford Diecast 1/43 scale model of Gumdrop (Ref: AHT001).
(Courtesy Oxford Diecast Ltd)

Val polishing Gumdrop at Cofton Park, July 2005. (Author's collection)

Proudly on display at The Royal Automobile Club, Pall Mall. (Courtesy the Royal Automobile Club)

Val's 1926 Austin 12/4 Clifton Tourer – named Gumdrop. (Author's collection)

Val sketching in his studio. (Courtesy the Enid Blyton Society)

The author, James Stringer, as sketched by Val Biro. (Author's collection)

four further versions of the Clifton tourer finished in Cobalt Blue, Maroon, Kingfisher Blue and Black, all of which were slightly different as they were based on actual cars.

Following *Gumdrop and the Farmer's Friend*, Val was to write a further 36 books featuring his well-known and much-loved Austin Clifton tourer. *Gumdrop's School Adventure* was the final Gumdrop story, written and published in 2001.

Sadly, on 4th July 2014, at the age of 94, Val passed away.

Chapter 2

The Austin village

It would need to be someone who was either blessed with remarkable foresight, had total trust in the loyalty of his workforce and absolute faith in what he was manufacturing, or a complete fool to commit such a vast investment in building an entire housing estate for the employees of a company barely eleven years old, and at a time when the entire nation was up to its eyes in muck and bullets, fighting for its very existence.

Herbert Austin, as we know only too well, was no fool, and he had the foresight to realise that, with the production of armaments in full swing at Longbridge, he needed to look to the future by securing a good and committed workforce for the time when hostilities ended, and pleasure vehicles would once again be driven through the main gates of Longbridge Works. He knew that for the company to survive, whatever the future may hold, it must look to its craftsmen and women, for it was they who were the most important assets it possessed.

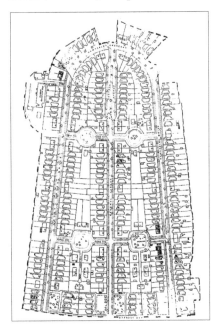

Providing housing for employees was not necessarily a unique or revolutionary idea, though. William Whiteley, owner of the London department store that bore his name, created the Whiteley village near Cobham in Surrey, whilst chocolate manufacturer George Cadbury did much the same for his employees at Bournville in Birmingham.

The idea of the Longbridge Estate was conceived in the main to ease the chronic housing shortage brought about by the Great War, where the workforce at Longbridge had increased from 2600 employees in 1914 to 20,000 by 1917, in order to cope with the high demand for armaments, military vehicles,

The Land Registry plan of the estate.
(Courtesy the Austin Village Preservation Society)

aeroplanes and aero engines. The demands and pressures of this work, together with the problems associated with transporting key workers to and from the factory, made living near their place of work essential.

On 16th November 1916, The Austin Motor Company purchased from Thomas Middlemore the freehold on 120 acres of land at Turves Green for the sum of £7750. The site was barely half-a-mile from the North Works, and comprised three farmsteads: namely Hawkesley Mill Farm, Tessell Farm and Longfield Farm, the latter having already been in use as a hostel for migrant workers from the city and as far afield as Belgium.

Once Herbert Austin had secured the land, he placed an order for 200 'ready-cut' Canadian cedarwood bungalows from The Aladdin Company of Bay City, Michigan, USA: a company recommended to him by Henry Ford. These were to be pre-cut and ready to assemble on-site. Such was their construction, it could be claimed that these structures may very well have inspired the prefabs of three decades later.

Each bungalow had a large living room measuring some 20 x 10ft; a kitchen of 10 x 10ft, fitted with a fixed dresser with cupboards, a drop-leaf table, gas cooker, gas washing boiler and a sink with a drainer; three bedrooms, each measuring 10 x 10ft; a bathroom and an inside toilet. The bungalows were heated by radiators connected to a coke-burning boiler, which also provided domestic hot water, and lighting was by gas ... and all for 18/- (90p) a week, inclusive of rates.

A enigma surrounded the roofs of these bungalows. Supposedly shipped separately in the hold of the RMS *Lusitania*, the roofs were 'lost' when the ill-fated vessel was torpedoed off the southern coast of Ireland by a German U-boat. The story, related by Zita Lambert in Bob Wyatt's excellent book *Lord Austin – The Man*, does not stand up to scrutiny, however, as the order for the bungalows was received by Aladdin Homes via a cable on February 1st 1917, whilst the *Lusitania* was torpedoed in May 1915.

In addition to the bungalows were 50 brick-built semi-detached houses, some of which were interposed between every sixth bungalow to act as a fire break. Whilst constructed to a fairly basic design, the houses – like the bungalows – were very well equipped: in addition to the fittings provided in the bungalows the houses had gas fires of 'the most hygienic kind' installed in the dining and living rooms. Both houses and bungalows came with gas light fittings complete with globes, and blinds, curtains and curtain rods.

The estate was laid out so that roads provided an east or west aspect for the

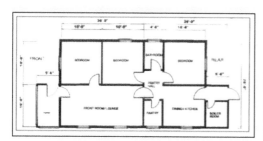

Plan view of the bungalow interior layout.
(Courtesy the Austin Village
Preservation Society)

Taken in the early 1920s, one of the
original residents standing by the front door
of her new bungalow. (Courtesy VAR Archive)

Above: Coney Green Drive shortly after construction.

Top right: The estate office and one of the children's shelters (inset).

Bottom right: Coney Green Drive showing the brick-built semi-detached houses.
(Courtesy *The Austin Advocate Magazine*)

bungalows and houses, and every property had a frontage of at least 10 yards. The roads were, in the main, straight and lined with trees, the major route being planted with forest trees (limes, scarlet chestnut, London planes, and oaks) along its entire length, whilst secondary roads were lined with rowan, maple, cedar and laburnum, all of which, with the exception of Hawksley Drive/Crescent, Central Avenue and Coney Green Drive, gave the 'avenues' or 'walks' their respective names.

Old farm buildings were converted into the Village Hall, where, as well as a club room, billiard room, ladies lounge, reading and card rooms, there was a concert theatre with seating for 350, all of which provided for the social needs of the community. Spiritual requirements were catered for by the provision of a Church of England Missionary Room, whilst non-sectarian worshippers were able to use the laundry mess room for gatherings. In 1921 a Baptist church was built on the land directly opposite Central Avenue, with Herbert Austin contributing £100 towards its cost, and performing the opening ceremony.

The laundry, erected on land to the north-west of the estate, was the only building equipped with an electric generator (Austin, perhaps?) which, as well as providing lighting for the laundry itself, also supplied the estate office, administration block and club buildings. The laundry had sufficient capacity to satisfy the needs of the estate, Longbridge Works, and many additional private dwellings.

Children of the employees were not forgotten either, with the erection of two large octagonal shelters in Rowan Way and Laburnum Way, and three additional play areas with swings and sand pits provided for the very young.

Work on building the estate progressed very quickly, with only eleven months between hammering in the first stake and occupation of the first property. 350 people

Top left: The club room.

Above: The billiard room.

Left: Herbert Austin at the official opening of
the Baptist church.
(Courtesy *The Austin Advocate Magazine*)

occupied the estate in the first years of its existence, and there was a waiting list in 1918 of over 100 names.

By the early 1930s the estate had developed into a thriving community, with the addition of local shops and its own newspaper. In 1929 The Longbridge Estate Association was formed to benefit the residents of the village, but was disbanded during the Second World War.

Today, over a century since the village was built, the houses and bungalows are mostly privately owned, but it still retains a strong community atmosphere. The estate association was re-established in 1990, renamed The Austin Village Preservation Society, which also revived the community newsletter. The village hall, now the Northfield Conservative Club, is still used for local events by the villagers, whilst the estate office, where the rents were once paid, has become an Indian restaurant, prior to which it served Italian cuisine. At the time of writing, (2018), the building was on the market for £325,000.

During 2018 the bungalows could be purchased for around £170,000, whereas one of the brick-built semi-detached properties in Central Avenue would cost in the region of £230,000.

It should be mentioned that Central Avenue was the very first ever dual carriageway to be seen in the UK.

The village is justly proud of its Austin heritage, and is now officially recognised as a listed conservation area. In addition to this, Birmingham City Council agreed to grant the wooden bungalows 'permanent building' status, after over 80 years of classification as temporary structures, with an estimated life of just 15 years.

In 2002 two blue plaques were unveiled in Central Avenue to commemorate the

Central Avenue showing the first UK dual carriageway. (Courtesy *The Austin Advocate Magazine*)

part Lord Austin played in establishing the estate and, of course, the vehicles that bore his name. To mark the centenary in 2017, the village was awarded £10,000 from the Heritage Lottery Fund.

The small saplings shown in the photographs taken in the early days of the village have now matured into full-size trees, and afford the estate a delightful charm that has to be seen to be appreciated. The children's play areas have, alas, not fared as well, and have long since disappeared, as has the Baptist church and laundry, which, under ownership of the Sunlight Company, was operating until the early 1990s.

Of the original 120 acres purchased for the estate, only 40 were actually developed. What became of the plans for further development was never recorded, but it is believed that with the difficulties experienced in getting supplies across the Atlantic at that time, further import of timber buildings may have been subject to an official ban imposed by HM Government; certainly no record exists of any further orders being placed with, or received by, the Aladdin Company.

All but one of the cedarwood bungalows and brick-built houses are still there: one bungalow being used by the erectors as a site hut accidentally caught fire and was destroyed. Without exception, all are maintained in an excellent condition and all are occupied.

The company that built the bungalows was founded in 1906: confident about the quality of its product, each bungalow came with a certificate declaring that for every knot-hole found in the outer cladding of the building, one dollar would be refunded to the occupier. It is understood that no knots were ever found, and no dollars were ever paid out! The Aladdin Company finally closed down in 1982, having produced 150,000 'ready-cut' buildings.

Two of the cedarwood bungalows as they appear today.
(Courtesy Rightmove estate agent)

Chapter 3

The Sizaire-Berwick

Imagine you are having a discussion with friends who share your enthusiasm for vintage motor cars, and you ask them what they can tell you about the Sizaire-Berwick Company. Chances are they will mention the shape of the radiator being the same as that of the Rolls-Royce, or maybe even the association with the entertainer Jack Waters (or Warner), who later became famous in the BBC tv programme *Dixon of Dock Green*.

However, it may not be as well known that at least two Sizaire-Berwick models were actually Austins with up-market coachwork ... but more on this later.

To clear up the matter of the Rolls-Royce radiator, Sizaire-Berwick *had* registered the design of its radiator in 1913, some time before Rolls-Royce. In fact, as it turned out, Rolls-Royce had not actually registered its design at all, so for the company to sue Sizaire-Berwick was not the best idea. However, after an amount of money changed hands, the matter was amicably resolved, with Sizaire-Berwick agreeing to alter the design of its radiator by making it slightly vee-shaped, and adding a narrow aluminium strip running down its centre line. This occurred just before the outbreak of the 1914-18 war, and the new design was put on hold until after the conflict.

On the matter of Jack Waters, or Warner, as he was later to become known, he left school and took up an apprenticeship in automotive engineering. In the August of 1913, when qualified, Jack was taken on as a mechanic and test driver by used car dealer and importer of La Licorne motor cars Fredrick William Berwick.

Berwick had premises in Highgate (North London), Acton (West London); an office and showroom at 18, Berkeley Street (London), and a workshop across the River Thames in Balham. At that time Jack lived with his parents and equally famous sisters, Elsie and Doris, in East London's Limehouse, which meant he had quite a journey across London to get to work each day.

Returning now to the Sizaire-Berwick story. At the turn of the century, the brothers Georges (20) and Maurice Sizaire (23) went into business to build motor cars; this they undertook in a small workshop in the suburb of Puteau, just to the west of Paris. They were joined in 1903 by Louis Naudin (27), and the company Sizaire et Naudin was formed as a result.

The business went from strength to strength, enjoying success in several French events such as the 1906 Coupe de l'Auto, a six-day endurance trial, and the Sicilian 1907

Louis Naudin. (Author's collection)

The Sizaire-Naudin driven by Georges Sizaire in the 1908 French Grand Prix, in Dieppe. (Author's collection)

Targa Florio. However, by 1913, Louis Naudin – who did not enjoy good health – died, and the brothers were left seeking a new partner.

In 1912, a Paris-based motoring journalist named WF Bradley had introduced the brothers to Fredrick Berwick, the London car dealer who, whilst deeply involved in the motor trade, was also very keen to manufacture motor cars himself: with the introduction to the Sizaire brothers, he could see that this may actually be the means to that end. Money, it would appear, was not a problem, as he had a wealthy backer in Alexander Keiller, the Scottish marmalade manufacturer. As a result the brothers agreed to go into partnership with Berwick, and the company Sizaire-Berwick (France) Limited was born and duly registered on 20th June 1913. The registered offices were based in Berkeley Street, London, with a new factory established in the Paris suburb of Courbevoie. It was agreed that at least 80 per cent of the chassis produced in the new factory would be shipped to Berwick's works in Highgate, where the bodies – which were of an exceedingly high standard – would be fitted by Berwick's own selected coachbuilder.

By 1914, Sizaire-Berwick had established itself as a company that produced exceptionally good motor cars using a proprietary 25/50 four-cylinder engine, about which a report in *The Field* read: "The most fastidious could not desire a better or more luxurious car for its power – nine out of ten motorists riding in one would accept it, with a sealed bonnet as a six-cylinder car. Nor does it suffer by comparison when inspected or dissected."

In fact, such was the esteem in which the Sizaire-Berwick was held that it was considered to be as good as the Rolls-Royce Silver Ghost, with, perhaps, better performance and also cheaper to run. Favoured by royalty and

M⁻. Naudin on the 6 Sizaire-Naudin car which attained speeds of over 60m.p.h. at Brooklands. Bore 100mm., stroke about 250mm.

Newspaper coverage showing Louis Naudin at the wheel of his car after attaining a speed of 60mph at Brooklands. (Author's collection)

heads of state, the President of France, M Poincare used a Sizaire-Berwick throughout the 1914-18 war, driven by Georges Sizaire.

At the onset of the 1914-18 war, Jack was sent to Courbevoie to collect a quantity

of Sizaire-Berwick chassis, which were then driven to England in threes, and put into storage at Highgate. These chassis were subsequently acquired by the government and fitted with armoured car bodywork for the Royal Naval Air Service.

A line-up of chassis awaiting shipment to Highgate. (Courtesy Martyn Nutland)

One of the chassis brought from Courbevoie in 1914 and fitted out as an armoured car. This did not prove at all successful, and was the only one ever built. (Courtesy *The World's Worst Weapons* by Martin J Dougherty)

After having invested in a very large factory in Park Royal (North-West London), with the intention of using it to manufacture Sizaire-Berwick motor cars, Fredrick Berwick's plans were put on hold due to the commencement of the war. However, on being awarded MoM (Ministry of Munitions) contracts, his new factory was used for the manufacture of de Havilland aeroplanes, and engines, lorries and armoured cars. The war had, in many respects, been good for Berwick, who had profited quite well from the MoM contracts, and, once the war was over, he could afford to re-jig this vast factory in order to return to motor car manufacture.

Berwick had his own range of coachwork, with names such as the Chiltern and Malvern torpedoes, the Chelsea landaulette, the Eaton limousine, and the Chelmsford cabriolet. Alternatively, customers could purchase a chassis and have coachwork fitted by companies such as HJ Mulliner. Prices ranged from £475 for just the chassis to £860 for the Eaton.

The Park Royal site, which covered 16 acres and employed 5800 staff, had the capacity to build 1250 cars a year, and with orders for £1.5 million already obtained, the post-war future of Sizaire-Berwick should have been secure. Alexander Keiller then decided to introduce his uncle to the company to oversee its future production.

In 1919, the company was floated on the London Stock Exchange with a £600,000 capital. Changes at the top saw Sir David Dalziel take on the role of Chairman, and he was joined on the board of directors by CJ Ford, who was also chairman of the Edison Swan Electric Company Ltd.

Maurice and Georges Sizaire, who were still involved in the building of motor cars at Courbevoie in France, travelled to England, bringing with them two draughtsmen. Maurice was very keen to continue with their pre-war design, which was still being produced at the Courbevoie factory. Berwick, however, wanted to introduce new models.

The war over, an optimistic advert appeared in ***The Autocar*** **of January 1919. Note the cheeky similarity to the Rolls-Royce radiator badge with the intertwined SB. (Author's collection)**

The company went ahead with a new design for the post-war market, designed by the two French draughtsmen, Voignier and Lapeyre. However, Keiller's uncle, who was also a steam roller engineer, decided to reinforce, thicken and make heavier almost every element of their design. So confident was he that his 'improvements' were correct, he went ahead and ordered sufficient material to manufacture one thousand motor cars without first even having built a prototype. The new model was a complete disaster and edged the company closer to receivership.

Later that same year, Keiller's Marmalade was taken over by Crosse & Blackwell, which wasn't interested in bank-rolling what, by then, was becoming a very sick car manufacturing company that was also involved in the manufacture of aeroplanes and aeroplane engines.

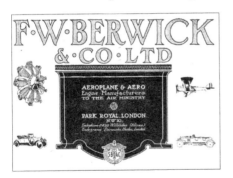

Three post-war adverts indicating the involvement in aircraft manufacturing at the Park Royal factory. (Author's collection)

Harvey du Cros.
(Author's collection)

By 1922, having produced just 250 motor cars, both Georges Sizaire and Berwick had left the company, with Maurice Sizaire departing a year later. Herbert Austin was approached to see if he could help the company in any way. The Austin Motor Company had itself only just come out of receivership, saved from annihilation by the 12/4 and, of course, the little Austin Seven.

Austin, together with Dubliner Harvey du Cros, came prepared to help in any way they could, providing they could profit by their actions. Du Cros had a well-proven history of acquiring companies both in the UK and France, and Austin saw this as a way in which his company could increase sales of the 12/4 and 20/4, and perhaps, if things did not work out well at Longbridge, acquiring a foothold in another car manufacturing company that he would be well-placed to buy into.

Herbert Austin and Harvey du Cros agreed to join the board of directors, and The Austin Motor Company supplied Sizaire-Berwick with the tried and tested 12/4 and 20/4 horsepower chassis, which would then be fitted with their own distinctive design of radiator and coachwork.

By October 1922, a new range of cars was launched. The 12hp Austin-inspired cars were marketed as the 13/26 at £450, and the 20hp as the 23/46 at £590. In addition was the 26/52, described as "An entirely new chassis designed by Herbert Austin." This turned out to be a three-litre, six-cylinder-engined chassis rated at 25.3 horsepower, and fitted with a three-speed gearbox. Whilst certainly bearing all the marks of being of Austin design, it had no counterpart in the then current range of Austin motor cars. The first six-cylinder Austin 20 was not to appear until 1927, with the 16/6 becoming available later that same year.

In the 1923 Olympia Motor Show, Sizaire-Berwick had just three examples on show, not including the 26/52 as this had by now been removed from the range. During the early part of that year only a few 26/52 cars, fitted with standard touring coachwork, were sold at a price of £1225. (It should be noted that a Bentley cost the same, and a Vauxhall 30/98 £5 less.)

By the following year the entire range of cars had been discontinued, and plans were made to replace them with just a single model for 1925: a 15hp (actually rated at 13.9hp) priced at between £695 and £835, depending on body style.

It is not recorded

The Austin 12/4 with Sizaire-Berwick coachwork and distinctive radiator (hidden by the radiator muff, regrettably). (Author's collection)

A side view of the 13/26 taken
from the SB catalogue.
(Author's collection)

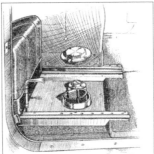

An image taken from the SB
catalogue showing the location
of the petrol filler cap, directly
under the driver's seat; exactly
the same as the early Austin
12/4s. (Author's collection)

An interior shot showing
the layout of gear and
handbrake levers on the
13/26. (Author's collection)

Out in the country, a 13/26 open tourer.
(Author's collection)

how many of these 15hp cars were actually sold, and there were never any road tests in the motoring press, but, later that year, the Sizaire-Berwick story came to an end.

Fredrick Berwick, after leaving the company, had become involved in the manufacture of the Windsor and British Salmson motor cars, and died in 1960. Maurice Sizaire, after leaving in 1922, went on to establish Sizaire-Fréres, and died on 28th January 1969 aged 92. Georges died just two years after leaving the company in 1924.

A 1923 25/50 two-seater
with dickey.
(Courtesy
Bonhams Ltd)

Chapter 4

Birth of a trademark

Herbert Austin's three young children were quite used to seeing their father draw strange and obscure images on the drawing board he had set up in one of the bedrooms at their home in Bearwood Grove. However, his youngest daughter, Zita, was fascinated by the curious-looking drawing that her father was currently working on, and, standing on tip-toe to obtain a better look, she asked him what he was drawing.

Herbert lifted Zita onto his lap so she could see the image more clearly, and explained that it was the design for a badge that would be fitted to the front of the motor cars he was making at his factory.

He then went on to explain that the image represented speed and motion that could be controlled: the two wings constituted 'speed;' 'control' was defined by the steering wheel, and 'motion' was represented by the road wheel and the whorls of dust being thrown up by it.

It is not known whether Zita, who would have been about five or six at that time, totally understood the significance of what her father told her, or what exactly it was supposed to mean, but what she witnessed that Sunday afternoon was the birth of one of the most iconic trademarks, recognised throughout the world as representing quality, dependability, and value for money.

Note: The emblem did not actually appear on the radiators until late 1907 or early 1908, though it was used as Austin's registered trademark in 1906.

Speedy – Controlled – Motion

Chapter 5

From stately limousine to charabanc

When UO 1477 left the Austin factory at Longbridge in early 1927, it was delivered to the Austin agents in south Devon as a very smart and luxurious Austin 20/4 Marlborough three-quarter landaulette limousine, finished in royal blue and black and priced at £595. It served its new owners well for the best part of ten years, by which time it was considered old-fashioned, and put up for sale, being replaced by a more up-to-date model.

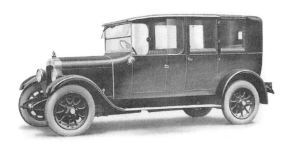

How UO 1477 would have looked when leaving The Austin Motor Company's Longbridge works. (1928 Austin sales catalogue)

UO 1477 was then purchased by the proprietors of the Sidmouth Motor Company, Mr Griffith and Bill Dagworthy, to be converted to a charabanc in which to convey holidaymakers up and down the steep, 1-in-4 gradient hills of Salcombe and Peak – the only routes by which Sidmouth could be reached.

Because of the Austin's low gearing, the Twenty was ideally suited for this type of work, once fitted with its new 13-seat 'toast-rack' charabanc bodywork, which was actually secondhand, having been salvaged from a 1912 Fiat requisitioned for war work. The Austin was considered fit to carry out its new duties, the conversion having been undertaken by Dowell's (coachbuilder) of Exeter.

A few minor modifications were carried out on the Austin, such as inserting two extra leaves to each of the rear springs, and fitting a transverse spring from one rear spring to the other. It was also fitted with smaller rear wheels to enable lower gearing.

The Sidmouth Motor Company ran its fleet of charabancs right up until the start of the 1939/45 war, when they were laid up until peace was restored to this quiet Devonshire seaside town, and holidaymakers returned. As the years went by it became necessary to have each vehicle inspected in order to retain the requisite Passenger Service Licences. The crunch came in the mid-1950s when the licences were revoked,

One of the other Austin Twentys, TT 5132, scheduled to motor up (and down) Peak Hill. (Courtesy The West Country Historic Omnibus & Transport Trust)

UO 1477 in the early 1950s. The newspaper covering the radiator is the *News of the World*, and carries the headline "Peace at Last." Could this be referring to the Korean war, perhaps? (Courtesy The West Country Historic Omnibus & Transport Trust)

simply because it was now considered dangerous for vehicles to have open sides, out of which, potentially, passengers could fall and be injured or killed. Mr Griffiths took the only option open to him and put his fleet of Austins up for sale.

UO 1477 was sold to the Vintage Passenger Vehicle Society's Museum in Exeter in 1956, with the remainder of the cars also finding new homes. In one guise or another, all are probably in existence today.

It's interesting to note that there was no timetable for these vehicles, and passengers were never really sure which of the hills they would be climbing. On one occasion a passenger did ask the driver which route they were taking, only to be asked, "Which one would you like to take?" As you might imagine, the charabancs generally drove very slowly up the hills, almost coming to a stop as double-declutching was attempted to reach a lower gear. This didn't go unnoticed by Sidmouth's younger generation, who frequently took the opportunity of hopping on for a free ride! It is understood that for a number of years one of the other 'toast-racks,' TT 5132, a ten-seater based on a 1925

UO 7095: one of the 'toast-racks.' (Courtesy The West Country Historic Omnibus & Transport Trust)

Austin Twenty, was giving rides around Bicton Gardens near Exeter.

UO 2331 had an enclosed body with a canvas roof made by Tiverton's (Coachbuilders) of Tiverton, and is now in store at the Colin Shears Museum in Exeter, after being purchased from The Sidmouth Motor Company for £30 in 1955 by bus enthusiast Brian Thompson.

UO 7095 (a 13-seater) was purchased by a Mr David Bygraves, who rallied it in the mid-1960s. It then passed through several hands, with the last sighting of it being rebodied as a touring car, the body since having been removed and refitted to a 1-ton Morris commercial chassis, when it was shipped to New Zealand.

Following several years in private hands, UO 1477 was repurchased by three local businessmen, Richard and Stephen Eley and Tom Griffiths, the grandson of Bill Dagworthy who had originally converted it to a charabanc. The Austin has since been totally restored by Tim Whellock and Tim Miller of Vintage Sports Cars at Chard in Somerset, and, at the time of writing is back once more in Sidmouth where it can be hired for special occasions.

UO 1477 seen parked in Sidmouth, now fully restored and affectionately known as 'Betty.' The car is available for private hire. (Courtesy The West Country Historic & Omnibus Transport Trust)

THE SIDMOUTH MOTOR CO. AND DAGWORTHY LTD.

*

PROMENADE COACH SERVICES TO PEAK HILL AND SALCOMBE HILL

*

SPECIAL DAILY TOURS TO ALL PLACES OF INTEREST BY ALL-WEATHER MOTOR COACH

———

FULL PARTICULARS FROM THE WESTERN GARAGE SIDMOUTH PHONE 318 & 644

The advertising board for the services offered by the Sidmouth Motor Company and Dagworthy Ltd, which began from the kiosk located at the esplanade car park.

Chapter 6

'OLD MIN'

On 28th May 1951, listeners to the BBC's Home Service sat down to enjoy the first of a new type of comedy programme, *The Goon Show,* the brainchild of Spike Milligan, co-written by Peter Sellers and Harry Secombe. This surreal comedy continued for eight series, finally ending in 1960.

The Goon Show introduced us to many different characters, which included Neddie Seagoon, played by Harry Secombe, Bluebottle and Major Denis Bloodnok played by Peter Sellers, and Minnie Banister, Eccles and Count Jim Moriarty played by Spike Milligan.

Spike Milligan owned a 1930 Austin 12/4 Open Road Tourer, purchased in 1950. For reasons unknown, he decided to name the car 'Old Min,' after the show's Minnie Banister character. The car was Milligan's pride and joy, coveted by Peter Sellers, who, as the owner of several Rolls-Royces, Aston Martins and a Cadillac, could be described as a total car nut.

Old Min when owned by Spike Milligan.
(Courtesy C Williams)

The Austin Twelve handbook.

Over the years, Sellers tried several times to purchase the Austin from Spike, even offering him 'silly money' in order to persuade him to part with it, but Spike was having none of it, even to the extent of rubbing Sellers' nose in it by phoning him to tell him what a marvellous time he had just had out with the family in Old Min.

However, things were to change. One night, following a performance at one of the many clubs, whilst driving home in Old Min Spike was invited to pull over by the boys in blue, and was offered a breathalyser. "I am afraid it's turned green, Mr Milligan," said the policeman. "Well, what do you expect," retorted Spike, "I am Irish!" Whilst Spike's answer may have raised a smile with the police officer, the Magistrate was less impressed, and Spike losy his driving licence for a year.

Not wishing to be tempted to drive Old Min during that period of enforced abstinence, he decided to offer the car to Sellers for the sum of £200. Sellers was, of course, delighted, and set about having it renovated, spending the sort of money on it that others could only dream of.

Peter Sellers standing next to his newly-restored Austin 12/4. (Courtesy C Williams)

Peter Sellers' fourth and last wife, Lyn Fredrick, turning over Old Min's engine. (Courtesy C Williams)

33

Once his year's ban was over, Spike found Old Min parked on his driveway, and closer inspection revealed a very expensive bottle of champagne on the front passenger seat. Although Peter Sellers retained ownership of the Austin, they both enjoyed many more outings in it together or with their respective families.

Some tine later, Sellers, on calling round to have dinner with Spike, was deeply upset to find that the Austin had been left parked outside, looking very sad and dusty and obviously quite uncared for: as if this was not bad enough, the radiator cap had been replaced with a coffee percolator lid! Whilst this had a profound effect on Sellers' feelings, the crunch came when Spike made a throwaway comment about an Oscar that Sellers thought he should have won. This insult – together with the condition in which he had previously found the Austin – convinced Sellers to sell the Austin, and he sent his chauffeur to Spike's to collect it.

Spike tried to buy the car from its new owners, but the asking price of £60,000 was just too much.

Old Min passed through the hands of several more owners. Forty years later, an advert appeared in *Classic Car Weekly* for an Austin Twelve convertible, that was believed to have been owned by Peter Sellers. The vendor lived in the Yorkshire Dales, and confirmed that, indeed, the car had been owned by Sellers, although he did not have conclusive proof to that effect.

Whilst conducting research into the history of the Austin, its new owner made contact with the person responsible for its restoration, who was able to fill many gaps in the car's history, and even put him in touch with the Sellers family, who said that they would love to see Old Min again. A date was arranged and the Austin was driven to Cobham in Surrey, where Old Min was reunited with the Sellers family.

Since first writing this chapter, it has come to light that Old Min was sold by Bonhams for £30,375 on 20th May 2021.

Old Min as she appears now. (Courtesy C Williams)

Chapter 7

The New Zealand earthquake of 1931

New Zealand is no stranger to earthquakes, as it rests on a major fault line in the Pacific Ocean, and experiences, on average, some 14,000 minor disturbances every year. Although very few are actually felt, around 20 or so do register over five on the Richter Scale.

In 2011, Christchurch, on the South Island, suffered a massive quake that destroyed much of the city centre, and almost totally annihilated the historic Anglican Cathedral built between 1864 and 1904 that was granted heritage status in 1985.

In February 1931 a very severe earthquake occurred in Napier on the North Island, in which 256 people perished. The quake, New Zealand's most deadly natural disaster, measured 7.8 on the Richter Scale, and struck at Hawkes Bay, causing 525 aftershocks that lasted a further two weeks.

This incident was reported in the May edition of the *Austin Magazine & Advocate* by Mr EC Lackland, owner of an Austin Seven Top Hat fabric-bodied saloon car, and who also provided the photographs for his story.

In his report, he commented that, for safety, he slept in the car at night, but was frequently woken by several aftershocks that caused the car to 'dance.' The initial earthquake occurred on 2nd February, and was followed ten days later by a second very big one.

Mr Lackland reported that the experience was most uncanny: "It seemed as though my two rear tyres had suddenly gone flat, and that the car was

Mr Lackland's Austin parked amongst the ruins of what once was a church. The Austin Seven parked behind it suffered badly from the falling debris. (All photos reproduced from the 1931 *Austin Magazine & Advocate*)

A section of the west shore road that leads
into Napier, and two vehicles caught at
the time when the road disintegrated.

The brave little Austin Seven, a trifle battered
and worn, photographed shortly after the second
quake.

slithering from one side of the road to the other. There seemed to be some unseen thing wrenching at the back of the car. The swaying of the telegraph poles soon forced upon me that I was in a big shake, and I can tell you that no stopwatch would have recorded the time it took to stop the car and get out!"

He then went on to say that he was a rotten sailor, referring to the heaving of the ground that resembled the waves of a rough sea. He ends by noting that the entire coastline from Cape Kidnappers up to the Far North was covered in a massive layer of dust from the falling cliffs.

It can be seen from the photographs that

A bad road slip 30 miles inland of Napier.
The size of the Austin Seven allowed it to
negotiate what was left of the road and
avoid the drop on the left-hand side.

the quake showed little or no respect for Austin motor cars (especially the Seven), and Mr Lackland's little Top Hat saloon car suffered along with many others, though it was probably lucky to have survived on this occasion.

The photographer's Austin parked
in the distance on one of Napier's
main streets, amongst some of the
devastated buildings located in the
business area.

Chapter 8

An Austin XII on the frontier

In 1935, a small paperback book was published by the Church of England Zenana Missionary Society, which recorded some of the humanitarian work being carried out on behalf of Indian womenfolk by a dedicated group of female missionaries in the province of Baluchistan, and which involved the use of an elderly Austin 12/4 Clifton Tourer as their only means of transport.

Baluchistan sits right at the entrance to the Khyber Pass, in what is now Pakistan.

According to the *Concise Oxford Dictionary*, 'zenana' is a Hindustani word for 'women,' and refers specifically to a room in a house where women of high-caste families can seek exclusion from men and visitors by simply drawing a curtain or purdah across the room's entrance.

Because of this exclusion, many Indian women were unable to obtain medical help when needed, as doctors were predominantly male.

Front cover of the book.

The Church of England Zenena Missionary Society was established in 1880 and, as well as missionary work, was deeply involved in education and the medical welfare of such women.

The book is written by Doctor E Gertrude Stuart, MB (Lond), and tells the story of the Society's work through the 'eyes' of the Austin. It begins:

I am an elderly Austin 12/4 – a 1924 model – now very old, but I have lived such a busy, and, in so many ways, full and interesting life, that it seems worthwhile to give some account of it.

My first owner was an officer who used to travel all over the frontier district to see how things were going in the outposts of the Empire. My second master was also an officer, but his battalion was stationed in Quetta Cantonment, so he did not go far afield. When he disposed of me I was given as a present to the doctor in charge of the Zenana Mission Hospital in the town of Quetta, and I was glad to hear that she found me a great improvement on the old car I succeeded, and which was a typical 'bone shaker.'

On visiting the patients, often in out-of-the-way places, the Austin had this to say:

The Doctor would be picked up from the hospital, then off we would dash at full speed with the Doctor at the wheel. When we got out of town, or off the military road onto the rough track which led to the village, I would leap and bound over all sorts of obstacles; through small streams and over river beds, where happily there was no water, but which had fearfully steep banks and pebbly bottoms. At last the road would come to an end and the man who had so far guided our course would seize the bags and hurry Doctor off to a mud dwelling, while I was left to my driver, who anxiously examined my springs and screws, and sometimes found that they were decidedly the worse for wear.

Dispensing
medicines from
the Austin.

The Austin was frequently required to carry far in excess of its recommended payload; the following extract covers just such an occasion.

I remember one day when I really had to remonstrate, but to no purpose, for in spite of my creaks and groans they packed into my back seat, on top of all the boxes of medicines, a pregnant woman and her mother, with the dispenser standing beside them and holding onto the back of the front seat; the woman's husband squatted on the luggage carrier, the driver sat on the running board and the two English ladies with more packages were in front.

Disasters – natural and otherwise – were a fairly normal occurrence in such places, but to an Austin Twelve an earthquake can be a very frightening experience!

When it came, I was resting in my garage one night when suddenly there was a terrifying shaking, not in one direction only – but first one way then another, then round and round. With a horrid crash the roof fell on me but evidently something kept part of the weight off of me, though my hood

was smashed up. The front wall of the garage fell out and when the horrible rumbling had subsided I heard the people who lived in the servant's houses round our compound calling out for help.

My driver, when he had time, came to see how I was, and found that I was less damaged than he

The hospital after the earthquake.

had expected, so with the help of a band of soldiers, and with much effort, they hauled and lifted me over the fallen wall and out onto the road – not that it looked like the usual road, for it was covered all over with fallen material from the walls of the houses. My driver found to his delight that I was still strong enough to be of further use!

The extremes of temperature that the elderly Austin was expected to endure are illustrated by the following extract:

How cold it was going out into the countryside during those winter days! I don't mind telling you that there were some mornings when I felt justified in refusing

Handing out blankets.

to start, but all sorts of people were called in to help, and they pushed so hard that I had to 'go'!

When a new vehicle arrived on the scene, the Austin felt just a little put out!

The Doctor got a new car with money given by the Red Cross Society, but though I felt rather hurt, I managed to hide my feelings. The chassis belonged to a new Chevrolet that had been damaged in the earthquake, and on it a contractor had built a little omnibus-like body. I considered that it looked clumsy, but even so it was a help for the ladies to have a covered car in the winter. One day the Chevrolet arrived back crowded, one might say over-crowded as one man had overflowed onto the roof! I couldn't help laughing at the sight, but my new colleague was very upset, and when we were together that night he grumbled a good deal. "It's not fair on a car's springs to pack it up like that," he commenced. "I was determined to show what I thought about it, so I refused to start for some time, then I thought of the sick people waiting to get here, so I relented, but even then I couldn't get up and down some of the steep ditches in the fields. The men had to get out and help, though I don't think they liked it." He chuckled a little as he described how they had pushed and dragged him along, I felt a bit superior. "Of course you're a heavy chap," I said. "Now, I am not as big as you, of course; I can get up and down obstacles." "Oh, like a tank I suppose," said the Chevrolet rather sneeringly. I realised he was jealous so kept a dignified silence, and soon he came round and told me how useful he was to Doctor, and I must say I agreed with him.

All too soon the Doctor and her sister returned to England, and, left alone with the Chevrolet for company, the Austin Twelve had these final words to say:

They all know that as old as I am, I shall go steadily on with my work for as long as people make use for me and are willing to just put up with the complaints that I cannot always suppress.

Notes

The earthquake referred to occurred on May 31st between 02:33 and 03:40 in Quetta, the capital of Baluchistan, now part of Pakistan. It measured 7.7 on the Richter Scale and accounted for the deaths of between 30,000 and 60,000 people.

As for the Austin Twelve, it survived and could even still be out there, somewhere on the frontier!

TA 929 was registered in Devon during the early part of 1924 to a serving officer in the 1st Battalion of the Queen's Royal West Surrey Regiment. When his regiment was posted abroad, he took the Austin with him.

Chapter 9

An artist's impression

The Austin Motor Company's Press and Publicity Office used many different methods to promote its products and bring them to the notice of the buying public. One such method used by the Company was to employ commercial artists to illustrate the latest ranges of motor cars, with beautifully-drawn, eye-catching watercolour paintings of the various models.

One such company was Hemsoll & Maxfield, a commercial artists' studio, situated in Temple Chambers, in Birmingham's Broad Street.

One of its earliest assignments was to promote the Austin Seven with a delightful poster showing a family comfortably seated in their 'Chummy' (registration number RU 41), seen driving past a similar family on foot, who can only look on with envy at the small but comfortable little car. The caption reads: "Don't Covet – Buy One." A similar illustration featuring the same two families has the slogan "Oh for an Austin Seven."

Douglas Maxfield aged 20.
(Courtesy Dr E Molem)

Don't Covet – Buy One. A poster showing an Austin Seven Chummy. (Courtesy Dr E Molem)

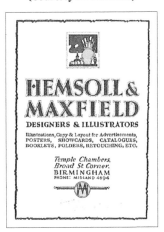

Advertisement for Hemsoll & Maxfield. (Courtesy Dr E Molem)

Another Austin Seven illustration shows a very wet and possibly windy scene, as the man who bears a remarkable likeness to Sir Winston Churchill is hanging onto his hat! The model on this occasion was a Top Hat saloon, in which we may assume the occupants are snug, dry and warm. However, this particular illustration is credited to Ben Smith, who, it is believed, may have been a pseudonym for

An Austin Seven Top Hat saloon braving a wet and windy evening. (Courtesy Dr E Molem)

Douglas Maxfield's wife, Margaret Noble, who was also an accomplished artist.

For 1930, Hemsoll & Maxfield was commissioned to produce a 10ft long frieze featuring the entire range of the latest Austin models for the dealerships to post around the walls of their showrooms.

The 10ft-long frieze showing examples of cars from the 1930 range, set against the background of *Widecombe Fair*. (Courtesy Dr E Molem)

The vehicles in question were the 20 horsepower, six-cylinder Austin Ranelagh limousine, a 16 horsepower six-cylinder Burnham and Iver saloon, a 7 horsepower Chummy, and a Seven Wydor fabric saloon. The frieze also featured a four-cylinder 12 horsepower Eton two-seater with dickey or 'rumble' seat. In-between the six illustrations was the script 'Austin Cars' with the company logo on each side.

The theme chosen for this publicity display was Widecombe Fair, and on each illustration, hidden amongst the shop names, was a reference to one or more of the characters mentioned in the song, such as Brewer, Hawke and Davey.

Two of the car illustrations from the frieze. (Courtesy Dr E Molem)

Three more details from the frieze.
(Courtesy Dr E Molem)

Left: The 1930 Austin 20/6 Saloon.

Below left: The 1930 Austin Seven Wydor saloon.

Below right: The 1930 Open Tourer Austin Seven.

Douglas Maxfield was born in 1893 to parents who were silversmiths living and working in Sheffield. The family enjoyed a good standard of living until an investment in a Swedish silver mine ended with a dispute over ownership, causing them to lose both their investment and family fortune. Following this, the Maxfield family moved to Birmingham, with Douglas, now in his early teens, becoming an auctioneer's clerk. By 1911 Douglas had enrolled at the Birmingham School of Art, where he studied for the next three years.

Following the outbreak of the 1914-18 war, Douglas volunteered for War Service, serving as a draughtsman with the Birmingham Battalion of the Royal Worcestershire Regiment. In 1920 he returned to art school to complete his studies, and it was during this time that he met his future wife, Margaret Noble, whom he married in 1926.

Douglas, together with his brother-in-law, Eric Hemsoll, had earlier set up a commercial art studio, whilst Margaret had already established herself as an accomplished watercolour artist specialising in book illustration.

During the 1930s, Maxfield & Hemsoll was kept busy designing eye-catching publicity material for many other automotive manufacturers, and companies as diverse as those producing golf balls and sauces, providing the Maxfields with a comfortable standard of living in their King's Heath home.

By the late 1930s, with another war just beginning, the Maxfields decided to take a holiday in Llandudno. Whilst visiting friends in nearby Conway they were shown a derelict cottage that, coincidentally, had always been referred to as 'Maxfield's Cottage.' Margaret fell in love with this and seriously considered making an offer for it.

After talking it over with Douglas' father, and with the bombing of Birmingham intensifying, the couple decided to purchase the cottage. By October 1940, they had moved their entire family to North Wales, thus bringing to an end the firm of Maxfield & Hemsoll Commercial Artists.

The cottage had no running water or electricity, but, in spite of this, they loved living there in the peace and tranquillity of the Welsh countryside. Sadly, neither Douglas or his wife lived long enough to see old age, with Douglas dying quite young and Margaret developing Parkinson's disease.

Some years after their deaths, their grandson and granddaughter decided to clear out the cottage; while undertaking this task, they came across a treasure trove of early Art Deco artwork and posters that had been hidden away behind panelwork in the upstairs attic bathroom. Sadly, some had suffered from the effects of damp, scorching, and attention from rodents, but the collection of original artwork showed what prolific artists the Maxfield's were, with examples of posters advertising Penfold's golf balls, HP Sauce, Singer motor cars, Velocette motorcycles and, of course, Austins.

Chapter 10

Sir Malcolm Campbell (1885-1948)

Sir Malcolm Campbell was a racing motorist and journalist who broke the world land speed record during 1924 at Pendine Sands, attaining a speed of 146.16mph. In all, he broke a total of nine land speed records between 1924 and 1935 in various vehicles, all of which he named 'Bluebird.'

His final record was broken at the Bonneville Salt Flats in Utah on 3rd September 1935 at a speed of 301.337mph.

Campbell also broke the water speed record four times, attaining a speed of 141.74mph on 19th August 1939 in Bluebird K4 on Coniston Water.

Campbell's love of motor cars is reflected in the photograph below, which shows him standing in front of his fleet of two Rolls-Royces, an Austin 16/6, and an Austin 12/4, which he had recently purchased for his wife. In an article published in *The Austin Magazine* of December 1929, he wrote: "The new model, both from a point of view of general performance and value for money, is the best proposition it is possible to buy on the market today. The 12hp Austin that I

Sir Malcolm Campbell. (Courtesy *The Austin Magazine*)

Sir Malcolm Campbell with his fleet of motor cars. (Courtesy *The Austin Magazine*)

Parked on the road to Verneuk.
(Courtesy *The Austin Magazine*)

have had since May last year is still running as well now as when I took delivery."

In this short recommendation Sir Malcolm does not say to which model Austin he is referring, but seeing as he mentions the 12 horsepower, it would be more than likely that it was the 12/4 Windsor Saloon, and not the later Burnham.

Capt Campbell also expressed great satisfaction with the 12/4 he purchased for his wife in 1928, stating that it had given admirable service. So maybe this was the car to which he was referring?

The first of the two photographs on this page shows him in his 12/4 Burnham saloon, when he was staying in Africa on the occasion of his attempt on the world speed record at Verneukpan. A comment on the photograph, taken on the road from Cape Town to Verneuk, notes that the signpost on the right of the picture was not manufactured from timber as one would expect, because if it had been it would have been stolen for firewood!

The second photograph, of the 12/4 Windsor saloon referred to above, shows Mrs Malcolm Campbell posing with the car on the day it was purchased. This photograph appeared in *The Austin Magazine* dated December 1928.

Sir Malcolm Campbell died on 31st December 1948, after suffering a series of strokes.

Mrs Malcolm Campbell with her new Austin 12/4 Windsor Saloon. (Courtesy *The Austin Magazine*)

Chapter 11

The Cambridge University Austin Sevens

In the 1950s, Austin Sevens were a familiar sight amongst the usual day-to-day traffic in and around the university city of Cambridge, for the model afforded a cheap reliable means of transport to the many undergraduates who studied there, and, besides which, it was fun to drive and easy to maintain as spare parts were plentiful and relatively cheap.

Such was the popularity of Herbert's little baby amongst the students a club was established specifically for owners within the university. The Cambridge University Austin Seven Club is still very active today, renamed the Cambridge Austin Seven & Vintage Car Club, and is now open to all owners of Sevens (and other vintage cars) living in the area.

PARKED UP ON THE ROOF ...

On the morning of Sunday 8th June 1958, those walking along King's Parade who cared to look skyward towards the roof of the Senate House saw a strange sight: parked on the rooftop was an Austin Seven van! Why was it there, and how on earth did it get there? More to the point, who was responsible for putting it there?

The prank was the work of a group of twelve engineering students led by Peter Davey and assisted by Cyril Pritchett, David Fowler and nine others. Originally devised the previous year, it wasn't possible to carry out the plan then due to it being too close to the end of term, However, by the following year the idea had developed to the point where it could now be put into action.

Although the roof of the Senate House was not easily accessible,

No double yellow lines here! The van parked up on the roof of Caius College. (Courtesy *The Cambridge Daily News*)

47

other than by bridging an 8ft gap between that and the roof of Caius Court (pronounced Keys), it was considered that if the apex of one building could be joined to the other with suitably placed planking, there was a good chance that access could be achieved.

The vehicle they intended to use was a 1930 Austin Seven van, which they had found axle-deep in nettles, and minus its engine. It was obtained for just four pounds, ten shillings, (£4.50), and sold to them on condition that the back axle and tyres were returned afterwards.

The lack of an engine was considered a bonus as the vehicle had to be as light as possible in order to make handling easy, and to not cause damage to the Senate House roof.

Now, with the purchase of the van there was no going back, and all the months of planning were soon to come to fruition. On the night of 28th May, a survey of the roof was carried out and a drawbridge of planks put in place from the roof of Tree Court to that of the Senate House. Calculations were made and measurements taken, from which scale drawings were drawn up to enable a derrick, using 'borrowed' scaffold poles, to be manufactured.

Pulley blocks, hooks, hemp and wire rope, carefully cut to the required length, coiled and labelled, were also acquired and stowed away in readiness.

Meanwhile, at a farm at nearby Coton the van was being lightened as far as it was possible, whilst still able to be steered when towed. A hole was cut into the roof, through which the lifting tackle could be passed and connected to a strong lifting eye, in turn attached to the chassis at its centre of gravity. The back axle was loosened so that it could be removed and returned to its owner. Fittings were then attached to the back of the van to take two short lengths of scaffold pole, which were to be used to move it into place in the manner of a wheelbarrow.

The method chosen to hoist the Austin onto the roof was via a 24ft high triangular derrick, constructed from the scaffold poles and arranged to overhang Senate House Passage. The apex of the derrick was held in place by a length of wire attached to a huge stone urn on the King's side of the building. This had a five-part block and tackle that could be shortened to pull the Austin inboard and over the foot-high balustrade.

On 4th June a trial assembly of the derrick was undertaken, and as this proved successful, the derrick was dismantled, folded up and stowed away out of sight.

All that now remained was for the van – which had been parked up out of sight – to be brought into Cambridge without raising suspicion: achieved by disguising it as a publicity vehicle. It was towed into Cambridge on Saturday 7th June, covered in enormous posters advertising the May Ball, and parked up by Clare College where the back axle and good wheels were removed to be replaced by an old axle and old wheels and tyres. The doors and rear wheels were removed, wrapped in brown paper and taken into Caius College disguised as pictures and cushions. The van was then covered in polythene sheeting and given a parking light.

The prank was planned to take place at 12.30pm, with personnel recruited for both ground and roof parties. Police beats had been monitored and timed, and look-outs arranged for an alarm: a Vespa scooter being started outside Great St Mary's Church, but the activities of a group of drunken revellers attracted the police and the alarm was sounded. An hour later than planned, the endeavour to park an Austin Seven van on the Senate House roof commenced.

The van was trundled into Senate House Passage, The roof party was in place and the derrick was made ready. The van was attached and the weight of it taken to raise it off the ground: at that point one of the joints slipped, having been insufficiently tightened, but once tightened, lifting resumed until it was about halfway up, when the six men doing the hauling took a short rest. At that point three drunken oarsmen from the nearby rowing club appeared and stood beneath the suspended van. They went on their way satisfied after being told that it was a captive balloon and that they could not have a ride on it.

Eventually, the van was hoisted above the balustrade, and the derrick was gently hauled inward. At that point it was found that the van was hanging awkwardly and would not pass between the narrow gap at the apex of the derrick and clear the balustrade. An attempt to swing it round was made, but it touched the derrick, causing it to tip backward. There then followed a thunderous crash as the van dropped about 5ft, and the derrick overbalanced onto the roof. Fearing that they would be discovered the lifting team quickly manhandled the van into place onto the apex of the roof, hastily dismantled their equipment and escaped over the plank bridge.

In the morning a crowd of onlookers had soon gathered to witness the unusual sight of a van parked on the roof, and stayed to watch as members of the Fire Brigade and Civil Defence battled with the problem of removing it. This task took just under a week to complete and, after several unsuccessful attempts at removing it in one piece, it was necessary to cut it up in situ and remove it piece-by-piece.

Whilst the Caius College authorities did not see the funny side of this escapade, and had no idea who the perpetrators were, the Dean of Caius, the late Rev Hugh Montefiore, had his suspicions. As a goodwill gesture, acknowledging the amount of work that had gone into the planning of this escapade, he sent a congratulatory case of champagne to the staircase of those he considered may have been responsible.

The perpetrators, who were never caught, went on to enjoy distinguished careers, and became generous benefactors to the college.

High and dry. A rear view of the 1933 Austin Seven van set against the Cambridge Skyline. (Courtesy *The Cambridge Daily News*)

Removal of the illegally parked van caused some head scratching. (Courtesy The Cambridge Austin Seven & Vintage Vehicle Club)

49

Left picture: Gently does it. Fire Brigade and Civil Defence members guide the van down towards the roof edge.
Right: Over she goes. Not an easy task but one that was finally achieved by cutting up the van and lowering it piecemeal. (Courtesy *The Cambridge Daily News*)

... AND THEN SUSPENDED UNDER THE BRIDGE!

Five years after the prank that saw the Austin Seven van parked on the Senate House roof of Cambridge University, another group of pranksters struck, only this time it was the university's famous Bridge of Sighs that drew their attention, using, yet again, an Austin Seven.

Ray Walker owned a garage in Perowne Street, which specialised in Austin Sevens – the make and model much favoured by students at the university as they were cheap to buy, cheap to run, and spare parts were plentiful. In fact, such was the popularity of the Austin Seven that the students had even formed their own club – The Cambridge University Austin Seven Club.

In the early 1960s there were usually a dozen or more 'Sevens' to be found on Ray's forecourt in various stages of repair or renovation, some were there for work to be carried out on them, and some were there to be sold.

At that time a half-decent late 1920s or early 1930s Seven could be purchased for between £5 and £10, or one with a current roadworthy certificate (an MOT) as much as £20.

It was one evening in June 1963, shortly before closing for the day, that Ray became aware of a group of five or six students looking at the Austin Sevens in the yard. They were showing a particular interest in an extremely rough looking 'box' saloon, which had no engine or gearbox, as these had been removed and sold for £5 to someone who wanted them for a speed boat. Ray had only paid £2 for the car.

Thinking that they were looking for something to run, Ray pointed out the deficiencies and the vital

A selection of Austin Sevens on Ray Walker's forecourt.
(Courtesy Gerald Walker)

parts that were no longer there, explaining that a lot of work would be required to ever get it running again.

"Oh, that's alright," said the one who appeared to be in charge. "We don't need it to have an engine or anything like that, as it doesn't need to run. How much do you want for it?"

With the Senate House roof incident still fresh in his mind Ray said, quite sharply, "Look, this isn't for some stupid prank, is it? Because if it is I'm having no part of it."

At this, the lads turned towards

Four further examples of Ray Walker's stock of Austin Sevens. (Courtesy Gerald Walker)

the gates to go and were just about to leave when Ray, seeing how disappointed they were called them back. He told them that he did not want anything for the car, and told them that if he came to open up in the morning and found that it had 'gone,' they, or anyone else would not hear any more about it.

Sure enough when Ray opened up the next morning he found that the car had disappeared. The next time Ray was to hear anything about the Austin was when he picked up the *Cambridge Daily News* to be confronted with the headline "SOMETHING TO SIGH ABOUT" with a picture of the Seven suspended beneath the Bridge of Sighs.

The feat was accomplished by roping a number of punts together on which they had mounted a platform strong enough to take the Austin. When it was secured, the raft was poled down the river and secured directly beneath the bridge.

Wire ropes were then passed through the windows from accomplices stationed on the bridge, and fed down to those waiting on the punts.

The centre of gravity of the car had been determined beforehand, and so when the ropes were secured to the car they were placed in the correct position to ensure that when released from the raft it would hang correctly under the bridge.

When the students were satisfied that the car was secured, the raft of punts was allowed to be floated out from beneath it.

The Austin Seven suspended beneath the Bridge of Sighs. (Courtesy the Cambridge Austin Seven and Vintage Car Club)

The prank was discovered quite early the following morning and the college authorities immediately set about releasing it from suspension. For this they borrowed one of the floating platforms from a nearby punt hire company that they used to bring the Austin back onto dry land.

The perpetrators, like those involved in the Senate House Roof incident were never caught, but of course there were those in authority who had a good idea who may have been behind it. The Austin was spotted shortly afterwards through the gates of what was believed to be property belonging to Lord Rothschild, but its ultimate fate was never known. Ray Walker was made an Honorary member of the Cambridge University Austin Seven Club, which now thrives as the Cambridge Austin Seven and Vintage Car Club.

The suspended Austin was removed very quickly from under the bridge.
(Courtesy Tom Johnson)

Chapter 12

The Brough Superior Austin BS4 (the Rolls-Royce of motorcycles)

When 29-year-old George Brough purchased premises in Haydn Road, Nottingham back in 1919, his aim was to manufacture the most up-to-date and probably the most expensive motorcycles ever made, following on from those manufactured by his father since the 1890s. The machines were intended to be superior to anything currently manufactured in Great Britain, and could rightly be considered the 'Rolls-Royce' of motorcycles.

That his motorcycles were costly but highly regarded by those who purchased them can be measured by Brough's customers, who included George Bernard Shaw and TE Lawrence (Lawrence of Arabia), who actually purchased six, but was killed in an accident involving one of his Brough Superior motorcycles, and never took delivery of his seventh.

Each machine was custom built to cater for the customer's needs, and therefore no two bikes were ever the same.

By 1924, Brough's yearly production had risen to 195, and seen the introduction of the Brough Superior SS100, which was guaranteed to achieve 100mph. The cost of each bike ranged from £100 to almost £200, which, at that time, was around the average annual wage for a man in Great Britain.

A superbly-presented BS4.
(Courtesy The Brough Superior Club)

By 1931, George was very keen to manufacture a motorcycle with a four-cylinder engine, and, rather than develop one himself, looked to the highly successful Austin Seven as a viable means of providing exactly what he was looking for.

An approach to the Austin Motor Company met with its approval and work began on designing a frame that would accommodate it.

The Austin Seven engine was rated at 747cc, which, in George's view, made it a little sluggish; it was uprated to 797cc by re-boring the cylinders by a further 1.9mm from 56mm to 57.9mm; by fitting the block with a light alloy cylinder head, he was able to

George Brough wearing his trademark flat cap,
sitting astride a Brough Superior Motorcycle.
(Courtesy The Brough Superior Club)

George Brough (standing, left) outside his
works in Nottingham.
(Courtesy The Brough Superior Club)

increase power output to 33bhp at 4600rpm. Just for good measure twin carburettors were added. The prototype cost over £1000.

Now named the Brough Superior Austin Four or BS4, the bike was powered via a normal Austin Seven transmission from the three-speed gearbox, including reverse, through to a shaft-driven pinion housed in a cast aluminium final drive unit, mounted between a pair of rear wheels spaced just 7½in apart.

From the outset the BS4 was intended to be ridden only with a sidecar attached (that George also manufactured), because with two rear wheels the bike would not handle the same as those with only one, particularly when cornering. However, one BS4 was ordered without a sidecar by Herbert Chantry, a journalist who had previously 'borrowed' a show model from the factory for use in the New Years Eve Land's End motorcycle trials of 1932.

From the outset the BS4 was never intended to be speedy, and in a 1931 edition of *Motor Cycle Magazine* it was described as a luxurious passenger outfit that would attain a speed of something better than a mile a minute for as long as road conditions allowed.

A BS4 combination.
(Courtesy The Brough
Superior Club)

One of the two
radiators fitted
to the BS4,
clearly showing
the Austin
'Wings & Wheel'
badge.
(Courtesy
The Brough
Superior Club)

The report on the BS4 that appeared in the *Motor Cycle Magazine* shows a cutaway illustration of the Austin Seven engine mounted in the bike's frame. (Courtesy The Brough Superior Club) *www.brough-superior.com*

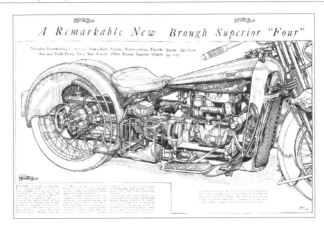

Only ten BS4s were built during 1932, with a further two in the early part of 1933. Of these, eight are known to exist today, with two in the USA and one in the Southwold Museum, New Zealand. However, as recently as 2015, a collection of Brough Superior motorcycles was discovered in a barn in Cornwall, which included the BS4 ordered by Herbert Chantry, and which was subsequently sold a year later by Bonhams the auctioneers for a staggering £331,900!

The BS4 discovered in a barn in Cornwall, subsequently sold by auctioneers Bonhams for £331,900. (Courtesy Bonhams Auctioneers)

To conclude this chapter it's fitting to include the following statement by George Brough. Asserting that the BS4 was a luxurious passenger outfit capable of over 60mph, George continued: "My ambition has been to produce a vehicle which has the charm and exhilaration that only motorcycling can give to the true enthusiast, whilst possessing advantages of silent running, effortless starting, cleanliness, and the more foolproof transmission of a thoroughbred car."

Footnote

George Brough died in 1970, but production of the Brough Superior had come to an end just before the start of the Second World War. Today, the Brough Superior name has been resurrected by Mark Upham, an Englishman, who has taken up where George Brough left off, and is manufacturing hand-built examples in Toulouse, France, which sell at a staggering £49,999 piece. But not, I hasten to add, with an Austin Seven engine!

Chapter 13

The tale of an Austin Eight

The Austin Eight was launched at the 1938 Motor Show at a time when Britain was about to become engaged in yet another war-to-end-all-wars. The Austin Eight was introduced to replace the Austin 'Big' Seven, which effectively brought to an end the Seven's long and popular run.

Pre-war Austin Motor Company advert for the Austin Eight. (Courtesy Tony Mealing)

A 1940 Austin advertisement for the 'military' Eight. (Courtesy Tony Mealing)

Once war was declared, the government needed vehicles to fulfil all manner of roles, and the little Austin Eight touring car was considered ideal as a lower ranks staff car; a contract was accordingly placed with The Austin Motor Company for a sizeable order.

The Austin Eight in this story was purchased under procurement contract 294A/502, dated 14th October 1939, and given the number AP 25152.

AP 25152, when delivered, was allocated to the Royal Army Service Corps (RASC), and shipped to France as part of the British Expeditionary Force.

As we now know, the BEF was to prove no match against the might of the German Army, and had to retreat to the coast at Dunkirk, abandoning all of their precious vehicles whilst they attempted to return home to England. In order to make the vehicles useless to the enemy, they were ordered to disable them in whatever way they considered appropriate. The usual way of disabling a vehicle was to remove the engine's sump plug and run the

An Austin Eight, similar to that in this story, on the way to France.
(Courtesy Tony Mealing)

Abandonment: Dunkirk 1940.
(Courtesy Tony Mealing)

engine at maximum revolutions until, well, it stopped! AP 25152 was either apparently considered to be of no great importance in this respect, or perhaps those who arrived in it were more concerned about boarding a ship as, after being driven onto the beach, it was simply left there, largely untouched, on the beach at Dunkirk, amidst the detritus that was once the pride of the British Army.

The fact that this little Austin was still in one piece, and therefore of use, was not

The German Chancellor, Herr Hitler, taking an interest in the latest Austin motor cars on display at the 1939 Berlin Motor Show.
(Courtesy Tony Mealing)

lost on the enemy, who removed it from the beach, repainted it Wehrmacht grey, gave it a new number and put it back into service, only this time for the other side! At some time during its new ownership the electrics failed and had to be replaced using Bosch parts. Once running again it continued to serve its new masters, moving from department to department from the Eastern Front and back into France; allocated different identification numbers from each department as it did so.

As the war progressed – and with the arrival of the Americans and return of a much-strengthened British Army – the conflict began to go badly for the Germans. The Austin Eight was forced to bid *auf wiedersehen* to its German masters, and was once more back with friends, only this time with the free French, who considered it ideal transport for the Fire Department.

Now painted bright red and with white upholstery, the little car was used by the Fire Chief, Monsieur Baril, as a personal runabout. The Austin was employed on a

Now in the hands of the Wehrmacht, its new owner delighted to be driving an Austin!
(Courtesy Tony Mealing)

Crossing a river, the driver and passenger don't seem too concerned that they could become stuck! (Courtesy Tony Mealing)

A similar car painted in red, recently photographed at a classic car event. (Courtesy Tony Mealing)

Now repainted white, and sporting Peugeot headlamps and bumpers from a Renault. (Courtesy Tony Mealing)

daily basis by Baril, but eventually, due to the car's age, it was stored in a garage and forgotten about. On Baril's death in the late 1960s, the car passed to his son, and was liberated from its long hibernation and quickly given a makeover: repainted white and used as his wedding car!

Over the years AP 25152 has experienced many changes, acquiring lights from a Peugeot van and bumpers from a Renault. Baril's son subsequently passed away and the car passed into *his* son's ownership. He was not all that keen to keep it, and sold it to his father's best friend, who, as it turned out, drove the car for him to his wedding.

In 2013 the car was sold to Charles Emmanuel Blanchet, who has taken on the task of fully restoring it to original condition, but would that be British Army Khaki, Wehrmacht Grey, Free French Fire Brigade Red, or even Black ...?

Chapter 14

'Mugwump'

On June 30th 1963, a 1930 16 horsepower, six-cylinder Austin Burnham Saloon car was driven to Dover from Bristol, to board a car ferry for what was to be the start of the longest journey this car had ever taken. Its destination was the South African city of Cape Town, and the car's occupants were four students from Bristol University. Three of the students were studying Engineering and one was studying Law; the latter invited along because, as his father owned two vintage Austin Twelves, and also an Austin 16/6, it was considered that he could be useful in that respect. The students were: Roger Freshman, aged 25, from Canterbury; Timothy Walford, 21, from Long Sutton in Somerset; Philip (known as Silas) Clegg, 21, from Blackpool, and Peter Chubb, 22, from Gloucester.

The idea of undertaking this trip came from Roger, who had only recently returned from a three-month-long visit to South Africa, and thought it would be quite an adventure to do the journey overland in a vintage motor car.

That they arrived at their destination was achievement enough, but students from the University of Cape Town were then offered the challenge of driving the car back to Bristol, covering a total of 23,830 miles in the process.

The Austin was purchased from two elderly spinsters who had owned the car from new, but had reached an age where they were no longer able to drive, agreeing to sell it to Roger Freshman for the sum of £60.

Roger and his team set about trying to obtain sponsorship for their journey; a task that initially met with very little positive response. That soon changed, however, when the late Lord Montagu of Beaulieu agreed to part-sponsor the trip with a donation of £1000, providing the car carried a board on the roof rack advertising the Montagu Motor Museum, and 'suggesting' that the Austin actually came from the museum, which, of course, it hadn't.

On deciding what the Austin should be called, the name MUGWUMP was agreed upon. This has several meanings, some of which are slightly derogatory. Originating during the American Civil War, a Mugwump is sometimes defined as an undecided person sitting on a fence, with his mug (face) on one side and his wump (rump) on the other: in this instance, however, it was simply an anagram of *"Montagu's University Group With Unlimited Means of Propulsion"*

Now, with Lord Montagu onboard, other sponsors came up with various offerings, such as a trailer, a roof rack, spares, camping equipment, medical supplies, film equipment, and, of course, food.

Mugwump was as original as cars of that age could possibly be, and the only modifications prior to commencing the journey were to fit an oil bath air cleaner, an oil filter and an extra fuel tank. The rear springs were strengthened with the addition of an extra leaf; the water pump was refurbished, and the car completely re-wired. A front bumper was fitted in order to protect the radiator, and a roof rack plus a couple of storage bins were fitted along the running boards; additions – together with a full service – that were undertaken at the Queens & Brighton Motor Company Ltd, the main Austin garage in Blackpool, which just so happened to be managed by Philip Clegg's father!

On Sunday 5th May, Mugwump was driven to Beaulieu where it attended the Vintage Austin Register's annual driving test and concours. Here, the group met up with the late Bob Wyatt, the Register's Hon Sec, who was able to provide them with the address of his brother, Alan, who lived in Khartoum, should they ever need somewhere to stay there.

THE ADVENTURE BEGINS

So, with that, the Vintage Austin Students Trans-Africa expedition (VASTA) was born and ready to go. From attending the VAR rally the car was driven to Bristol, where it spent a few weeks in the showroom of Henley's Garage until the June 30th date of departure. The Austin was then driven to Lord Montagu's apartment in London, where the students were treated to an excellent farewell party, then, seen off by a group of parents, friends and well-wishers, the Austin's starter was pressed, the engine roared into life and Mugwump headed down the A2 towards Dover to board the ferry to Calais.

The late Lord Montagu of Beaulieu with Mugwump prior to the start of its journey to Cape Town. (All photographs of the outward journey courtesy Roger Freshman)

While motoring through France, an ominously loud bump-bump noise emanated from deep inside the engine. Parked up in a field, the engine was stripped to investigate the noise, only to find absolutely nothing wrong. The engine was re-assembled and, on giving it a test run, it was found that the noise had completely disappeared.

Continuing the journey through France and into Spain, upon reaching Lucena, a small village south of Madrid, the car experienced its first major breakdown. Mugwump had begun to backfire a little while previously, which gradually worsened until the engine finally expired. Removal of the cylinder head revealed that three exhaust valves had burnt out and needed to be replaced from their stock of spares. Working on the Austin in the village square soon attracted a group of local youngsters curious to know what was going on, thinking it funny to pretend to run off with their tools!

By 11th July the car had reached Gibraltar without further mishap, and boarded the ferry to Tangier. From Morocco, they headed east along the coastal road, through

A group of curious children gather around Mugwump in a village south of Madrid, whilst new exhaust valves are fitted to its engine.

In the mountainous region of Southern Spain.

Algeria, Tunisia, and Libya, and on into Egypt. Approaching the Tunisian border the car experienced its next major breakdown when the engine suddenly stopped: the timing chain had broken. Luckily, they had a spare chain and, after protecting the engine with blankets from the effects of a sandstorm blowing in from the desert, they were soon on the road again, first to Tripoli, then through the desert to Benghazi, which they reached on 24th July. From Benghazi they travelled to Tobruk; once again driving through the desert, eventually arriving at Sollum in Egypt. Getting through customs took two hours due to having to fill in a multitude of forms in triplicate before being allowed to cross.

The students arrived in Alexandria on 29th July, a month after leaving the UK, and decided to spend a few days relaxing at a seaside resort owned by the Egyptian Automobile Association. It was here that Philip began to complain about acute stomach pains, subsequently diagnosed as appendicitis. On arrival at Cairo he was admitted to the University Hospital, and operated on the following day. As his convalescence was for three weeks, the other three students took the opportunity to do some sight-seeing, which, of course, included the great pyramids at Giza.

Further to the financial help given by Lord Montagu, the BBC decided that an expedition of this magnitude would make an excellent documentary, and loaned the team the equipment to record their adventure on 16mm film, with a promise that if it was good enough, it would be given airtime on national television. Peter Chubb was to be the photographer, and he started off with great enthusiasm. As the journey progressed, however, his enthusiasm began to wane, especially since Philip's appendicitis had delayed the expedition by a month.

Their next destination was Sudan, intended to be

At the base of the great Giza pyramids.

61

via road. This was not possible, however, due to the construction of the Aswan Dam, so a boat was sought that would carry them on the Red Sea to Port Sudan, where they eventually found an old steam ship leaving Suez, upon which Mugwump could be loaded for the journey. The ship's captain was insistent that they join him in finishing off the bottle of brandy that was kept in the ship's medicine chest 'for medicinal purposes.'

Mugwump was then transported by rail from Port Suez to Khartoum, as the route by road would have taken them through desert they were not permitted to travel.

Driving alongside the Suez Canal.

Driving through the city of Mogren, they decided to call on Bob Wyatt's brother, Alan.

Alan recalls that, on hearing a knock on his front door, he was surprised to see the group who had just arrived in a 1930 Austin motor car. Their request for an overnight stay was, of course, granted and they were made comfortable on the flat roof of the property. Alan told them that, whilst his house was quite large and airy, it was built from a mixture of local bricks and cement, and was infested with scorpions. After three nights the lads departed, leaving a comment in Alan's visitor's book: "1st September 1963 – The all-time cadgers" (scroungers).

From Khartoum they drove the short distance south to Kosti, where again they made use of public transport by loading the Austin on to the Nile ferry to travel the 750 miles to Juba. This was to be a very slow trip along the Nile, taking ten days in the company of crying babies and bleating goats, whilst they slept next to Mugwump. The barge was attached, along with eight others, each side and in front of a paddle steamer, rendering the flotilla very hard to steer against the quite strong current of the White Nile.

Nearing the end of their ten-day voyage, the team decided to investigate a problem with Mugwump's compression, which, much to the amusement of their fellow passengers, meant stripping the engine and replacing an inlet valve.

From Juba, which is near the Ugandan border, they continued their journey through Uganda, Kenya, and on to Nairobi, where Philip Silas left to fly to Bristol for his final university year. As the other three members had finished their degrees, the delay was of little consequence to them, except that now, of course, they were a man short. Travelling via the Great North Road to Tanzania, they discovered that Tim, who had not been feeling too well for some time, had contracted jaundice, and was advised to leave the expedition and fly home to rest. The team, now further reduced to Roger Freshman and Peter Clegg, continued through Tanzania and on into Zambia, then Rhodesia (now Zimbabwe), where they were greeted by the Mayor of Salisbury.

From Rhodesia they had good tarmac roads, enabling them to make up some lost

Meeting the Masai locals in Amboseli, Kenya.

time when finally arriving in South Africa. The final leg of the journey took them through Pietermaritzburg, the Transkei, and along the Garden Route into Cape Town, where they were greeted by a cavalcade of vintage cars, driven out to escort them to the Town Hall where a reception had been arranged to welcome them. It was here, too, that they were introduced to the four students from Cape Town University who had volunteered to drive Mugwump back to Bristol. The four undergraduates were: Dunbar (Dan) Acutt (Rhodesian), Count Victor Szechenyi (Rhodesian), Nicky Taylor (South African), and Kevin Quick (Rhodesian).

With a herd of elephants for company the Austin motors on through Amboseli, Kenya.

The journey from Bristol to Cape Town had taken just under four months, and they had covered a distance of 11,806 miles (19,000km) at an average speed of 40-45mph, and a fuel consumption of 20 miles to the gallon. Mugwump, by now, was running very well, and the two British students managed to cadge free passage to the UK on cargo ships operated by Safmarine.

In the shadow of Mount Kilimanjaro: the Austin with bonnet sides removed to prevent the engine from overheating. (The headboard displays 'VASTA Expedition 1963' VASTA standing for: Vintage Austin Student Trans-Africa.)

63

At the Kariba Dam, Zimbabwe.

A chance meeting with another Austin of the same vintage outside Salisbury, Southern Rhodesia (now Zimbabwe).

In addition to the breakdown and repairs already described, there was also a broken shock absorber arm, a worn distributor drive gear, one burnt-out inlet valve, a worn propshaft fibre coupling, and eleven punctures.

With regard to filming the journey for the BBC, initially, the project worked well, but filming with heavy hand-held equipment proved very hard work for Peter, especially when taking shots of the car driving along stretches of road in the African heat. Peter would have to go on ahead with camera and tripod to film the Austin driving up to and then passing him, often in a cloud of dust, and then would carry all the equipment along the road to catch up with the now-stationary vehicle, as the trailer made it very difficult to reverset. When there were four team members, one or two of the others would, of course, have been able to help with this, but now reduced to just the two of them, Peter had this to do this alone.

The film was eventually made, but, on submission to the BBC, was not found to be suitable for broadcasting, regrettably.

THE RETURN JOURNEY

(Note: The Cape Town University students' return trip to Bristol followed much the same route taken by the students from Bristol University, and they therefore shared

many of the experiences encountered. This is especially noted with regard to when Mugwump was transported by ferry or barge.)

After discussing with the two Bristol students what route to take in returning Mugwump to Bristol, it was agreed that they should ask BMC (British Motor

A cartoon by Jackson of
The Argus depicting Mugwump's journey.

Corporation) to loan them a four-wheel drive vehicle, and travel up the West Coast of Africa, through the Sahara Desert to Morocco. This route would require a back-up vehicle, and, as BMC had recently started marketing the Austin Gypsy, BMC's version of the Land Rover, they suggested that BMC loaned them one for the trip. They considered that the resulting publicity would be excellent, as the Cape Argus newspaper was keen to send a young reporter to join the group, who would submit weekly progress reports and provide a full account of the Gypsy at the end of the trip. The returning group would be the four Cape Town students plus the two Bristol students and the reporter.

The four students from Cape Town University who drove Mugwump back to Bristol.
(L to R): Dan Acutt, Victor Szechenyi, Nick Taylor, and Kevin Quick.
(Photographs of return journey courtesy of Victor Szechenyi, unless otherwise stated)

However, after an initially enthusiastic response to their request, BMC then took three weeks to think about it, after which it rejected the idea on the grounds that should the Gypsy fail and the 1930 Austin complete the return journey, the resulting publicity would be very damaging for the company. Such was BMC's lack of faith in the reliability of the Gypsy that production of this vehicle ceased not long afterwards! However, prior to their departure, BMC did give Mugwump a major overhaul, including fitting new inner tubes to the tyres, which turned out to be slightly too big and were to necessitate several of the 46 repairs that the team had to carry out en route. In the event, the South African students decided to take a route similar to that travelled by the Bristol students, although, as it worked out, they were advised to cross the Mediterranean from Egypt into Italy, and thence through Europe to the UK and Bristol.

On December 2nd, following a reception held in their honour at City Hall hosted by the Mayor of Cape Town, they were seen off by Roger Freshman, Peter Chubb and representatives from The Crankhandle Club (the veteran car club of South Africa based in Cape Town).

Nick Taylor giving Mugwump a final polish before setting off.

Driving out of Cape Town.

The start of the return journey: Mugwump on the outskirts of Cape Town.

They had barely travelled six miles (10km), when they experienced the first of many punctures. This was fixed with the two Bristol students looking on, and, to their amusement, when the Cape Town students climbed back into Mugwump, they drove off leaving the trailer behind, having unhitched it to sort out the car's rear tyre. Several more punctures were to occur before crossing the border into Rhodesia (Zimbabwe). The car, which had been running well since leaving Cape Town, was now misfiring, and was taken to a garage in Salisbury (now Harare) to have this investigated. Whilst there, they were able to collect new tyres and tubes that had been flown from the UK by Dunlop. Up to that point they had suffered 26 punctures en route.

On December 14th they resumed their journey and were escorted out of Salisbury by cars from the local vintage car club; however, before long, Mugwump began to misfire again.

About to cross into Zambia, they were almost hit by two angry rhinos, who charged out of the bush chasing each other. The Zambezi river was crossed at Chirundu via a huge suspension bridge, after which they roused considerable curiosity from local tribesmen. As they progressed, the car began to suffer from fuel starvation, which was rectified by cleaning out the carburettor and the Autovac that fed it with petrol. It then began to overheat, the water in the radiator boiling as they drove up a steep incline, necessitating they stop to let the engine cool before continuing on to the border with Tanganyika (Tanzania).

At the border they found it was closed for lunch, so had to wait until lunchtime was over before being allowed to enter. It was here that they experienced some very

A short stop before crossing the Zambezi River. (Courtesy Andrew Quick)

Crossing the Zambezi via the suspension bridge at Chirundu.

Left: Mugwump approaching the quagmire in which three buses became well and truly stuck.
Right: The Austin, of course, managed to get through the quagmire with no trouble at all.

Making a few new friends on the way. The boards attached to the roof rack were changed to reflect the return journey (Cape Town STARVA EXPEDITION 1963 Bristol)
Note: STARVA stood for: Student Trans African Return Vintage Austin.

heavy rainfall, which caused the dirt roads to become very boggy, as evidenced by three buses that had become bogged down and could not proceed any further, The Austin did manage to get through, however, as the journalist from *The Argus* reported:

"The rain-soaked roads, which, at one point, claimed three heavy buses, proved no match for Mugwump. The Trans-African Austin, driven by four students from the University of Cape Town, although up to the axles in mud, the old but powerful engine had little difficulty in pulling the car through between the buses, which lay partially blocking the road."

By now the group had completed a quarter of the journey, and the students were able to take in the beauty of the Rift Valley, where they encountered a number of very friendly natives. At first a little unsure of Mugwump and its passengers, the natives were nevertheless amused by the sound of the car's klaxon horn.

On December 18th they set up camp at Mbeya, and the following morning found a garage to repair a leak in the car's radiator, along with further tyre punctures.

By the 21st, almost at Dodoma, a loud scraping noise was heard coming from the trailer, and it was discovered that the axle had broken, causing one of the wheels to rub against the trailer's bodywork, shredding the tyre until it was useless. The trailer was unhitched and the Austin, together with the broken axle, was driven the four miles into

Dodoma, where a new tyre was purchased and the axle welded, and two more punctures repaired.

A couple of days later they reached Pienaar's Heights, approached via a very steep hill, where they decided to make camp. On leaving here the following day, they heard the familiar scraping noise that indicated the trailer axle was again broken, only this time they were able to save the tyre from being shredded. They were now about 117 miles (188.2km) from Arusha and the nearest garage.

On arrival at Arusha they put up at a hotel for the night, and in the morning found a garage that, thankfully, did an excellent job of repairing the axle. They also collected some mail, which included a letter from the German consul in Nairobi inviting them to spend Christmas with him and his family. As it was then Christmas Eve, there was no time to hang about, and they continued on to Nairobi at speed. In their haste, after repairing yet another puncture, they almost collided with three giraffes and a hyena. After some time trying to find the consul's residence in the dark, they eventually arrived at 11.30pm, and, after a few very welcome beers, retired to the luxury of clean sheets.

They stayed with the consul and his family for a few days, enjoying a welcome

rest, good food, and very good company. When it came time to leave, the consul's wife advised them to take great care, as where they were heading was considered very unsafe. She gave them a Berretta .32 gun, which they gratefully took and stowed safely inside the springs of the back seat rest.

On December 27th they headed into town to apply for visas and to have Mugwump serviced. Then, after a farewell lunch, they departed for the town of Nakuru, 100 miles (170km) further on, and to the home of Sir Michael Blundell

Awaiting the return of the trailer's axle.

MBE, a prominent politician and farmer, where they spent the night.

Mugwump was, by now, running well again, and with no punctures to slow them they crossed the equator and drove on into Uganda, where they had supper at Jinja before motoring through Kampala to spend the night at a local campsite.

Whilst in Kampala they sought to book passage on a boat from Juba to Kosti, being unable to drive as the high level of the Nile was making the road impassable through the Sudd, a massive papyrus swamp. The following week was spent waiting for their booking to be confirmed, and on December 31st the group saw in the New Year with a night out in a bar of dodgy reputation, drinking copious amounts of beer.

Still without confirmation of their booking, they decided to press on towards Kampala. The Austin's fan belt had broken earlier, giving cause for concern, but the matter was resolved by having the top pulley skimmed to accommodate a modern belt. Whilst in Kampala they were able to obtain confirmation of their booking, and with a good tarmac road they were able to make up lost time as far as Bombo. On the journey they came across an area where bananas were grown, so stocked up with a giant bunch of green 'lady fingers' that they stowed on the roof rack under the tarpaulin.

Finding a decent place to set up camp for the night, just outside of the Murchinson Falls game park, they feasted upon provisions purchased in Kampala. During the night Victor and Nick were awoken by Dan indicating that they should quickly leave the tent and get into the car as quietly as possible, where Kevin had already taken refuge. Dan had spotted a massive bull elephant just a short distance away, wandering towards their camp, obviously attracted by the smell of the bananas. After a little while, the elephant moved off and Victor and Dan decided to return to their tents, leaving Kevin and Nick in the car. A short time later they were again awoken to find that the elephant had returned, and all four once more took refuge in Mugwump.

In the morning they checked over the camp to find elephant footprints indicating that in his quest for food he had quite remarkably stepped carefully between the tent's guide ropes without damaging them.

Their next destination was the Ugandan/Sudan border. The car was running well and by midday they had arrived there. Clearance to cross was quickly given, but after leaving they had difficulty locating the Sudanese border post, which turned out to be some 31 miles (50km) further on.

Arriving at the Sudanese border post two-and-a-half hours later they found it closed due to a 'terrorist' incident somewhere on the road to Juba, discovering that several of the people waiting to cross had been there for over a week. Wondering whether to abandon the trip, or drive all the way back to Mombasa and get a ship from there to Egypt, they made friends with the two border guards, who invited them in for a drink – which turned out to be the nearest thing to fire water that they had ever tasted!

The following day they were advised that a meeting had been set up to resolve the issue, and that the Sudanese Army Commander would be flying in by helicopter. The news caused a somewhat festive mood at the post, with the guards donning their best uniforms to await his arrival. An hour or so after the Army Commander's had arrived, Dan – unanimously chosen as spokesman – attempted to persuade him to let them through; in this he was successful, and was told that they could leave the following morning.

The group set off in a convoy, with Mugwump, as the slowest, leading a Jeep, an army lorry containing 30 soldiers, and 6-8 other cars, arriving safely in Juba, where they headed for immigration and customs for clearance, and were allowed to set up camp in the customs yard. Their impression of Juba was of a remote, desolate, dusty and ugly town, unbearably hot, with the largest and most vicious mosquitoes on earth.

By Friday 11th January, clearance had been obtained, and the cost of £150 for the passage paid for with cash provided by the bank. By 2pm Mugwump was ready to be loaded on the *Hurriyah* (Freedom): a most precarious operation, as this was not a single boat, but actually a collection of barges lashed together, three abreast, and driven by a paddleboat, which had accommodation for the crew. Other barges contained the toilets and sleeping accommodation, with bunk beds stacked three high, and mattresses stuffed with kapok; thin as a knife edge and filthy dirty.

As they watched other passengers board, complete with chickens and goats, the decision was made for to sleep on the open barge with the Austin. Their departure at 5am was without incident, except to find that they were in the middle of the Sudd – a large swamp area full of floating vegetation. The channel of clear water through which the *Hurriyah* had to sail narrowed to such an extent that it frequently became caught in the flotsam of papyrus and other vegetation. Barges that became stuck had to be released from the paddleboat and left to float down the river until they could be retrieved and re-attached, adding several hours to their journey.

The *Hurriyah* made several stops en route, picking up many locals going about their business, plus more chickens and goats, together with the menfolk, naked bar bead corsets and headwear, and women coated in red ochre. The smell that accompanied them made the travellers glad that they had decided on the open barge for the journey, although as this did not possess a toilet, they had to use that on the third class barge, treading through water, urine and faeces, plus the blood and entrails of animals, slaughtered for fresh meat, to get there. The smell, of course, was unbearable, and they found ways to access the toilets on the first and second class barges to avoid this awful experience.

On 20th January, after having been on the water for nine days, they disembarked at Kosti, where the task of unloading the Austin began. A steam crane, built in 1820, had insufficient power to lift Mugwump off the barge, even after building up a good head of steam. A second crane of similar vintage was brought in, and together they succeeded in lifting the Austin and lowering it onto a flatbed railway wagon for the next part of its journey to Khartoum, where the White and Blue Niles merged.

The journey to Khartoum went without incident, except that, it being the holy month of Ramadan, the train made several stops so that Muslims could disembark to pray. One elderly worshipper was so intent on his prayers that the train moved off without him; he chased after the departing train, which, when realising it had lost a passenger, eventually stopped to allow him to climb onboard. On arrival at Khartoum the students booked train tickets to Wadi Haiffa, to board a boat to Aswan,

The train departed at 6.45am and they settled down in a compartment occupied by other European passengers. As the train picked up speed it became enveloped in a thick cloud of dust that blocked out the scenery through which it passed, and necessitated keeping the windows firmly closed, making the compartment overwhelmingly hot.

On arrival at Wadi Haiffa the students inspected Mugwump, which looked to be in a deplorable state with dust covering everything, inside and out. The question now was when could the Austin be removed from the flat wagon and transferred to the steamer? Initially, to their dismay, they were told that the steamer did not take cars; then later advised that they would have to wait for the locomotive to return in order to move the car. They eventually found a ship that would take Mugwump, but which would not be departing for at least ten days: back in the marshalling yard they set about cleaning the Austin in readiness for departure.

Their activities were soon spotted by the headmaster of a local school, who took pity on them and allowed them access to his school, where they were able to sleep, shower and wash their clothes, which by now had become – well, very dirty, let's say.

The ship, or, to be more precise, barge, transported scrap, which, once loaded, allowed Mugwump to board. The Austin was to be joined by two Land Rovers and a Chevy pick-up truck, each of which the students had encountered earlier on their journey north.

Before they could depart they had to be cleared by customs, and were told that duty had to be paid at the rate of half a per cent of the value of the car, which, in the case of the Austin, did not amount to very much, happily. Loading was completed by

It took two ancient steam cranes to offload the car from the Hurriyah at Kosti.

Mugwump in mid-air, being hoisted out from the Hurriyah.

4.30pm on 30th January, and the barge moved to the berth from which the cars could be loaded, but did not come alongside. When this was queried, they were told that as it was Ramadan the labourers had ceased work for the day, and that customs was not prepared to supervise the loading.

Loading went ahead the following morning. First onboard were the two Land Rovers followed by the Austin, and then the Chevrolet pick-up truck, which almost came to grief when one of the planks gave way due to its weight, causing the truck to lean heavily to the right, threatening to topple into the Nile. The driver decided to give the vehicle a sharp burst of acceleration, which caused it to leap forward, landing fair and square onboard. The barge finally set sail once customs had given permission at 12.15pm.

Arriving at Shellal quite late after travelling along the Nile for seven days, unloading was postponed until the following day, when they were able to leave and await the customs officers arriving at 9am by train from Aswan. However, when the train did eventually arrive three hours later, there were no customs officers, and they were told that customs officers did not come to Shellal. The cars could not be unloaded without customs clearance, harbour police told them, though later suggested that clearance could be obtained at Aswan at 8pm that evening.

By now the barge had been moved around the wharf and the stevedores who controlled the loading ramps were demanding £5 per ramp per car. Refusal to pay this exorbitant charge resulted in much haggling, and the sum of £2 eventually agreed. They were then free to travel on to Aswan, accompanied by the captain of the barge, the facilitator (harbour police), and the owner of the ramps, who required

Another day, another ferry. Mugwump being driven very carefully onto the Nile ferry en route to Shellal.

paying in Egyptian pounds. They spent an hour at immigration, then went on to customs, where they informed the officer that waiting outside was the plank owner and the facilitator who each required paying, and asked whether he considered this to be fair? Without a word the officer went outside, and they heard him telling those waiting there for payment to clear off in no uncertain terms, from which they gathered that he did *not* think this to be fair!

On leaving Aswan, now driving on a freshly tarred road that was good for the first 40 miles, they were able to make good progress. After this point the road deteriorated into a rock-strewn surface, causing two tyres to burst in quick succession, Nevertheless, they made Luxor by lunchtime, and were able to visit the Valley of the Kings, and the tomb of Tutankhamun. Unlike Roger Freshman's party, who were able to scale one of the pyramids, the Cape Town students could only view them from ground level as climbing was not allowed.

Their next stop was Quena, where they were advised that the tarred road to Suez – formerly only accessible to the military – was now open to civilian traffic. Two more punctures were repaired before they reached Suez at 4am, and it was then on to Cairo three hours later.

At the Turkish Maritime Office they were able to book berths on the *M/V Karadinez*, scheduled to sail from Alexandria to Naples a few days later on 13th February. The cost of this was £100. With the help of the Egyptian AA (Automobile Association), customs was cleared very quickly, and Mugwump was hauled onboard, and safely secured on the deck.

As the *M/V Karadinez* left port, the African continent gradually faded and Europe hove slowly into view. The winter trip across the Mediterranean was very choppy, and Nick, suffering from sea sickness, had to spend much of the voyage in his bunk. Although the ship was of recent build, the berth had accommodation for over 100 steerage class passengers on bunks two-high. The urinals were at the front (bow) of the ship, clogged with, amongst other things, orange peel, causing them to overflow. It proved impossible to reach them without walking through the overflow, and the stench was so bad that the other students took to sleeping in the car out on deck.

Arriving in Naples on 16th February, they motored on to Rome where they were able to take in the famous sights, such as the Trevi Fountain, the Vatican, and the Colosseum. After spending the night in a monastery, they headed on to Pisa and climbed to the top of its famous tower.

They continued on to Genoa and the Alps, where they had their first encounter with snow. Next came Grenoble, and on through France, not stopping other than for fuel and refreshment, and finally arriving at Calais where they caught the ferry to Dover.

From Dover they drove to Canterbury where they met up again with Roger Freshman, who invited them to stop there for the night. In the morning, accompanied by Roger, they travelled to London, where a reception had been laid on for them at Lord Montagu's London apartment. Just before arriving there, Mugwump suffered two more punctures that, of course, had to be repaired.

All dressed up. Parked in front of a pyramid at Giza.
(Courtesy Andrew Quick)

After the reception in London, Mugwump was driven to Bristol: escorted by members of the local vintage car club, the car arrived safely at the university.

The Cape Town University students suffered no major breakdowns other than having to repair 46 punctures due to the new, ill-fitting tyres given to them by a benevolent sponsor in Cape Town. In due course, Mugwump was safely returned home after covering what amounted to 23,830 miles (38,350.6km).

Today, more than half a century on, Mugwump, is still very much alive, and after enduring several more remarkable journeys, is now back in Cape Town, being cared for by Mike Stuart, a prominent member of the The Crankhandle Club, the South African organisation for Veteran and Vintage vehicle enthusiasts. Roger Freshman, the leader of the original expedition, also lives very close to where the car is now kept, so can keep a paternalistic eye on his reliable old Austin 16/6.

After reaching Naples the group headed north for Rome, where they took in the Colosseum and the Vatican.

Enjoying the snow-covered Alps in Genoa.

Arriving in London, even more punctures required repair.

Nick Taylor, Victor Szechenyi and Kevin Quick pose with Mugwump.

Two Cape Town and two Bristol University students with Mugwump parked outside Lord Montagu's London Apartment. L to R: Roger Freshman (Bristol), Victor Szechenyi (Cape Town), Nick Taylor (Cape Town), and Tim Walford (Bristol).

Arrival in Bristol was greeted by members of the local Vintage Car Club.

**Kevin Quick and Nick Taylor on Mugwump's roof after arriving in Bristol.
(Courtesy Andrew Quick)**

**Mugwump now, living in South Africa.
(Courtesy Roger Freshman)**

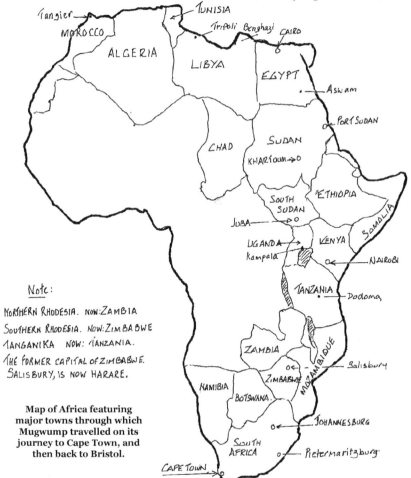

Note:

NORTHERN RHODESIA. NOW: ZAMBIA
SOUTHERN RHODESIA. NOW: ZIMBABWE
TANGANIKA NOW: TANZANIA.
THE FORMER CAPITAL OF ZIMBABWE.
SALISBURY, IS NOW HARARE.

Map of Africa featuring major towns through which Mugwump travelled on its journey to Cape Town, and then back to Bristol.

Chapter 15

Austin in receivership

At 11 o'clock on the 11th day of November 1918 the guns finally fell silent, and with that the war was over.

And so, too, ended the government contracts that, for the previous four years, had provided The Austin Motor Company with work that necessitated an increase in its workforce from just over 2500 employees to 22,300. No longer was Austin required

to manufacture armoured cars, shells, aeroplanes, gun limbers and ambulances with which to feed the insatiable war machine, and the Company could once again concentrate its efforts on what it did best before the outbreak of hostilities – producing good quality motor cars.

Top left: Horse-drawn gun limbers (1603 built). (Courtesy John Baker, *Austin Memories*)
Above: Armoured cars (480 built). (Author's collection)
Left: RE fighter planes under construction (120 manufactured). (Courtesy *The Austin Advocate Magazine*)

Henry Ford was a good friend of Herbert Austin, and had discussed with him the advantages of concentrating production on just one model, such as he had done with his Model T. Herbert Austin had given this advice some thought, and, even before the war began, had developed the car he thought would suit this objective very well.

⅔-ton lorries (52 built). (Author's collection)

The Austin Twenty had proved quite an outstanding motor car during the 1914 Austrian Alpine Trials, and although not winning the event, did give an excellent performance, demonstrating and re-affirming its quality of design and build. It was therefore this car that Austin decided he would concentrate his efforts on, once the war ended.

The Austrian Alpine Trial Austin of 1914. (Author's collection)

During the latter part of the war, Herbert Austin was often seen at the wheel of a Hudson Super Six, which, although of American manufacture, was considered to be a well-designed and engineered motor car, and more than likely played a part in influencing the design of the 1919 version of the Austin Twenty.

The Twenty, unlike its predecessors, had the gear and handbrake levers centrally positioned, the same as the Hudson, whilst the word 'GAS' appeared on the steering wheel's hand throttle control lever – all very American.

An illustration of the 1919 version of the Twenty (designated the P1), as published in the 1918 edition of *The Austin Advocate Magazine.*

However, the war had irrevocably changed many things during those four terrible years. No longer could owners of large motor cars afford to employ a chauffeur to drive and maintain the vehicle, and the cost of purchasing one was also a deciding factor. In 1917, exactly one year before the war ended, Austin published details of the Austin Twenty in the *Advocate Magazine,* and suggested that the price for the touring car would be around £400. In the event, the initial

One of the first adverts for the 'new' Austin Twenty touring car, as portrayed on a Company brochure. Note the slightly raised rear portion of the bodywork that was designed to hide the hood when opened. (Author's collection)

price was £495 for the Tourer, £595 for the Coupé, and £625 for the Landaulet, plus purchase tax at 33⅓ per cent.

The Austin Twenty was launched at the 1919 London Motor Show, and it was hoped that, once production got into full swing, the Company's future would be assured. Indeed, sales were going very well, with orders initially outstripping supply, though at that stage the Company was not completely ready to produce the number of vehicles required: some 25,000 vehicles a year, whilst the most that could be produced each week amounted to just 150.

Mass production on the scale of American motor car manufacturers was still very much in its infancy in the UK, and it was to take several years for many companies, including Austin, to completely re-tool to compete with the Americans in this respect. However, Herbert Austin was a very shrewd businessman and, not wishing to rely solely on the Austin Twenty, he considered several other options, such as aeroplanes, ⅔ ton lorries, tractors, and domestic lighting generation sets.

The (P2) Twenty on the road in 1920.
(Courtesy *The Austin Advocate Magazine*)

What actually was required, of course, was an upsurge in demand for the Austin Twenty. Regrettably, this did not happen, even though there was an enormous demand for new cars at that time: not, though, large 3.5-litre cars such as the Twenty.

Matters were not helped by the postwar slump, and scarcity and cost of raw materials. As if that wasn't bad enough, industrial unrest at Longbridge had drained the Company of well over a quarter of a million pounds.

A further factor that may have influenced the public's decision not to buy larger engines was the change in road tax fees. Up until 1920 the Austin 20 was classified as 'not exceeding 26hp,' and carried an annual tax of just £6.6.0 (£6.30). For 1921, however, the Chancellor of the Exchequer changed the method of taxation to an annual fee of £6 on all motor cars up to 6hp, and then, for every additional hp, an additional £1 would be added, thus making the annual tax for an Austin Twenty £23; constituting a massive increase of £16.14.0 (£16.70).

By 1921, the Company's financial situation had deteriorated to such an extent that, at times, there was insufficient cashflow to pay employees, and daily postal deliveries to the factory were eagerly awaited to search through for cheques that would help to keep the Company solvent for a little longer.

Herbert Austin was forced to decide whether to struggle on or close the Company. Calling together his senior managers, he explained how serious matters had become: taking a half-crown coin (12½p) from his waistcoat pocket, he announced that, with the toss of this coin, the future of The Austin Motor Company would be decided. Heads it would struggle on and Tails would mean imminent closure of the Longbridge factory.

The tossed coin came down showing the head of King George V, and the managers all breathed a sigh of relief. The coin was later inset in the office wall panel directly behind Austin's desk, where it remains to this day; a poignant reminder of how close the car industry came to losing the name of Austin.

Herbert Austin then called together all of his workforce and told them what had been decided that morning, asking that they work with him to overcome the current financial situation, even to the extent of a wage cut. The news was received with considerable relief, and the general agreement was to accept reduced pay packets for at least a

**The coin that Herbert Austin tossed to determine the future of the Company, now inset in the panelwork of his office.
(Courtesy A Osborne)**

**Lord Austin's office.
(Courtesy A Osborne)**

**The entire Longbridge workforce being addressed by Herbert Austin.
(Courtesy VAR Archive)**

couple of weeks so that the Company could sort itself out; indeed, a large number of employees made it known that in order to support Herbert Austin, they would actually go without wages until matters improved.

Herbert Austin's response to this was to promise his workforce a job for as long as The Austin Motor Company remained in business, and even into the 1960s there were employees working at Longbridge who had attended that meeting.

On April 26th 1921, Sir Arthur Whinney was appointed as receiver and manager, with the task of restructuring the Company and returning it to solvency.

By May 15th he had called a meeting of creditors, at which he suggested that they might be paid via second debentures to be paid from the Company's profits when available, which could be within just five years. This was agreed to and the threat of compulsory winding up was withdrawn.

By 16th March the following year, a court order was made approving the scheme that placed the affairs of the Company back into the hands of its directors, who were Herbert Austin (Chairman), Harvey du Cros (Deputy Chairman), CRF Englebach OBE (Works Director), EL Payton (Financial Advisor), Sir Arthur Hardinge, AT Davies, and TD Neal FCA.

Englebach, as works director and Payton, the financier, were to be largely responsible for restoring the Company's fortunes.

It was, of course, during the period when the Company was in receivership that Herbert Austin launched the Austin Ten, later to be known as the Austin 12/4. Finance for building this smaller version of the Twenty could not be sanctioned by the receiver, so funds had to be raised by selling off unwanted plant and stock. By the middle of 1921, permission had been given to go ahead with the prototype, and work progressed very quickly. By the time the receiver had left Longbridge, the 12/4 was in production, and, with glowing reports in *The Motor*, the future of the smaller version of the Austin Twenty was assured.

Adjusting the tappets on the prototype 12/4 chassis. (Courtesy *The Austin Advocate Magazine*)

Prototype 12/4 chassis on road test. (Courtesy *The Austin Advocate Magazine*)

An artist's impression of the prototype 12/4 chassis out on test.
(Courtesy *The Austin Advocate Magazine*)

Whilst this was getting under way, Herbert Austin was also putting in place the production of an even smaller motor car of just 7hp, that, together with the 12/4, undoubtedly helped restore the company's fortunes.

Chapter 16

The takeover bid by General Motors of America

Across the Atlantic, General Motors of America and Canada had its eye on the once-buoyant and well respected motor car manufacturer that had only recently bounced back from insolvency, and considered that, if offered the right financial incentives, it could be in the market for a takeover bid. So, early in 1925, negotiations began for the acquisition of The Austin Motor Company, with a view to adding it to GM's growing portfolio of motor car manufacturers.

There were those within the Company, including Austin himself, who were all for becoming a part of General Motors, and, providing the price was right, would have been agreeable to a takeover, but realising that news of such a move may not find favour with its shareholders, it was agreed to keep the matter under wraps until talks had become well advanced.

However, all was revealed when, in an edition of *The Motor* magazine, dated 8th September 1925, there appeared an article entitled 'GENERAL MOTORS AND AUSTIN,' that went into detail of an offer that had been made to acquire the Company, and of its provisional approval by the majority of the Board of Directors, with the exception of three, who were strongly opposed to this. The article read:

"After a week of indefinite and contradictory rumours it is possible to state that negotiations have been proceeding between certain representatives of the General Motors Corporation of New York, Detroit and elsewhere, and The Austin Motor Company Limited, with a view to reaching an agreement in the matter of an offer made by the American concern.

"No official information has been given as to the exact nature of the offer, but late on Thursday a statement was issued to the effect that, at a meeting of the Board of Directors of the Austin Motor Co Ltd, held in London on Wednesday, a resolution was passed approving provisional agreement to be entered into between Sir Herbert Austin, Chairman of The Austin Motor Co Ltd, and Messrs Morgan Grenfell and Co, acting on behalf of the General Motors Corporation, and that a scheme of arrangement for giving effect to the agreement and reorganizing the present capital structure of the Company was approved and recommended by the Board."

It was further stated that steps were being taken to place the proposals before the shareholders, and that nothing definite could be done without their, and the Court's, agreement.

The official announcement led to the assumption that the Board was unanimous in its approval of the scheme, but on the Thursday concerned, a statement was issued by three members of the Board of The Austin Motor Company Ltd – Messrs Theodore D Neal, Ernest L Payton (Finance Director), and CRF Engelbach (Works Director) – which said that, in order to avoid any misapprehension, the three found it necessary to state immediately that they were not in agreement with their colleagues, as they considered the American offer quite inadequate, and the terms of the reorganisation of the capital unsatisfactory.

When the offer and the scheme were put before the shareholders the dissentient directors issued a further statement, setting out their reasons for not recommending that they accept either the offer or the scheme.

In the meantime, circulars had been issued to shareholders, calling upon them to sign a form appealing to the directors to convene an extraordinary general meeting of the Company to consider, and, if thought fit, adopt a number of resolutions that had been drawn up before negotiations with General Motors were known to have begun.

As given in a later report issued on 30th September 1925, the full list of directors of The Austin Motor Co, Ltd were recorded as follows: Sir Herbert Austin KBE (Chairman), Harvey Du Cros (Deputy Chairman), Randle George Ash, Theodore D Neal FCA, Ernest L Payton, Sir Arthur Hardinge KCB, Alfred I Davies, and C F Engelbach OBE (Works Director).

The offer made by General Motors was subsequently rejected by the shareholders, and The Austin Motor Company was able to carry on trading as an independent British company.

During an interview some time later, when Sir Herbert Austin was asked why he did not 'marry the American lass,' he replied:

"Well, her dowry was quite substantial, but my relations did not like her, and therefore the engagement had to be broken off. I thought that it would be safer for me to marry her than someone else; also that co-operation would have been better than competition. The future might prove that I was right, but as the scheme has been abandoned, I have resolved to do everything humanly possible to prove that all the agents and friends of the company will assist me in the task."

That the takeover by General Motors never took place is, of course, history, but it is interesting to consider where the Company may have been today had GM's offer been accepted. General Motors, thwarted by refusal of the Austin shareholders to endorse the agreement, had to look elsewhere for a British motor manufacturing company to purchase. That it chose Vauxhall, which is still trading under its own name today, provides food for thought, perhaps ...?

Chapter 17

Herbert Austin on 'How to use a file'

During a short visit to England by his uncle, the young Herbert Austin became intrigued by his stories of adventure, and also of the many opportunities that were available to a young lad such as himself in Australia. His uncle was the manager of an engineering company in Melbourne, and more or less promised Herbert an apprenticeship under his guidance if he cared to return there with him.

Herbert did not need a lot of persuasion in this respect, and with his parents' blessing took his uncle's advice and joined him in Melbourne shortly after he returned there.

Herbert Austin was in his late teens when he started work at his uncle's engineering company, learning various skills such as simply filing a piece of metal to within several thousandths of a inch of its required size: skills that were to stand him in good stead when, several years later as manager of his own company back home in Longbridge, he could demonstrate to those whom he thought were in need of a little helpful guidance how certain tools should be used.

It was a well-known fact that 'The Old Man,' as Herbert was later affectionately known, was quite capable of undertaking any task carried out within the Works, and it was this fact that led him to observe the method being employed by one of his young engineering fitters whilst on his daily walk around the factory workshops.

The engineer in question was carefully filing a component with a smooth flat file in such a way that Austin felt the lad needed to be shown how the file *should* be used, in order to obtain the best results. So, taking the file from the lad's hands, he proceeded to demonstrate the correct way to use it, Taking the handle of

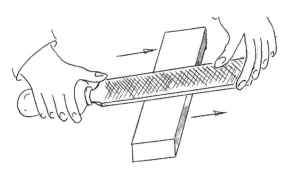

The 'correct way' to use a file.

the file in his right hand, with his left Herbert steadied the other end, gently pushing forwards and back at a slight angle, removing a small amount of metal each time.

The demonstration over, Herbert suggested the lad should always use his files in the way he had just shown him, and with that continued his walk around the Works, happy in the knowledge he had imparted good engineering advice to one of his employees. In reality, however, he had just ruined a perfectly good component part, and totally flabbergasted his employee, who needed only to take off a few thousands of an inch to complete the component, and was using a method known as draw filing to achieve this.

Draw filing requires the file to be held with both hands around its body, and then gently pushed forwards over the surface to be filed, thus allowing the smallest amount of material to be removed in a totally controlled manner.

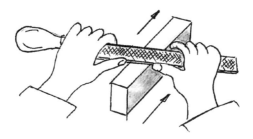

The method known as 'draw filing.'

Chapter 18

The dependable Austin (Seven)

T he slogan "The Dependable Austin" was frequently used in Austin publicity to suggest to the buying public that Austin motor cars were well-designed, well-built, and could therefore be relied upon perhaps more so than those from other manufacturers.

Whilst we have discovered in previous chapters that this certainly rang true with the Austin Twelve and the 16/6, it has to be said that the Austin Seven must wear the crown where long distance driving and dependability is concerned.

In August 1928, New Zealander Hector McQuarrie set off from Sydney in his Austin Seven named Emily to circumnavigate the world with his companion Richard B Matthews, in a series of adventures that covered a total distance of 22,000 miles. The car had been donated by the main Austin dealership in Sydney, where their journey began, in return for valuable publicity for the Austin Seven.

Their first adventure took them right up to Cape York in Northern Queensland, which they reached on 31st October. The journey covered 1300 miles, 700 of which were off-road. During this first leg they experienced having to drive through dense bush, patches of quicksand, crocodile-infested rivers, and forest fires, and also suffered, on average, 25 punctures *every day*.

Their next trip with Emily was in New Zealand, travelling from the top of the North Island to the bottom of the South Island.

The travellers then planned to ship Emily to San Francisco on the *SS Tahiti*, which would take three weeks to get there. However, that was not to be, as shortly after leaving Wellington on 18th October 1930, the ship's tail shaft broke, causing the propellers to drop off. The engine room flooded and the ship sank, taking Emily with her to the bottom of the sea. Fortunately, all 128 passengers and crew had time to abandon ship, and no lives were lost.

Hector McQuarrie and Richard B Mathews about to set off on their round-the-world trip in Emily. (Courtesy *The Austin Magazine*)

By March 1931, Hector and Richard reached America, and with a replacement Austin Seven named Emily II, continued their journey, visiting Britain, France, Italy, Yugoslavia, Bulgaria and Turkey, where they were fired upon by a Turkish soldier and also charged at by an unfriendly camel. Then it was on through Czechoslovakia, Iran, Syria and India, and finally back to Australia.

Also in the 1930s, Gladys de Havilland, sister of plane-maker Geoffrey (of Tiger Moth and Mosquito fame), somehow persuaded Herbert Austin to give her a new Austin Seven in which to drive around the world – good publicity I suppose! She covered much of the same route as had Hector McQuarrie in his Austin Seven.

Gladys de Havilland arriving in Picton, New Zealand accompanied by a large number of well-wishers, all in their Austin Sevens.
(Courtesy *The Austin Magazine*)

Coming slightly more up-to-date, we have John Coleman, who, in 1959, set out to drive the 11,000 miles from Buenos Aires to New York City in his 1925 Chummy. His epic journey was totally supported by The Austin Motor Company, which, at that time, was part of BMC, and made spares and the services of their agents available along the route. John's journey was not without its problems, as described in his book *Coleman's Drive*, published in 1962. Shortly after leaving the Argentinian capital, he skidded on soft tar, toppling the car and hitting a car coming in the opposite direction. He carried on, after being told never to stop after an accident, the Austin having suffered only minor damage, fortunately.

*****

We now bring our story of long journeys in an Austin Seven to more recent times when, in January 2013, five members of the Austin Seven Club decided to re-enact the journey undertaken by John Coleman 54 years earlier, and ship three superannuated Sevens to Argentina, with the intention of driving them to Times Square in the centre of New York.

Jack Peppiatt was no stranger to driving around Argentina in an Austin Seven, and, having read John Coleman's book and met him on several occasions, decided that he, too, would like to attempt such a trip.

Jack ran the idea past the owners of two Austin Sevens to see whether they would like to accompany him in their cars, and was delighted when they agreed to do so.

The team consisted of Diane Garside and River Dukes in their 1929 Chummy named 'Feisty,' Stan Price in his 1932 RN saloon named 'Dusty,' and Jack, together with his partner, Amanda Peters, with their 1933 RP saloon named 'Bertie.'

After much planning, and having given the three cars a thorough overhaul, they drove in convoy to Tilbury Docks, where they loaded the cars onto a Ro-Ro ferry scheduled to arrive in Buenos Aires one month later.

The drivers arrived by plane on 6th February, a little ahead of their cars, giving them time to sightsee as guests of the Buenos Aires Antique Car Club. They collected their vehicles on 20th February, and were seen off at the start of their journey by a group of well-wishers from the club.

Waiting to board the ferry at Tilbury in thick snow, 21st January 2013.
(All following photos courtesy Jack Peppiatt)

Plaza del Congreso, Buenos Aires. The Parliament building, 20th February 2013.

The first leg of their journey took them to Santiago, where they stayed at Estancia San Ramón, a property belonging to a friend and fellow Austin Seven owner, then across the flat pampas towards their first major challenge – crossing the Andes – which took three days to accomplish, covering a distance of 130 miles and an ascent of 7682ft to reach the summit pass. Fortunately, thanks to a new road tunnel that had been built since John Coleman's journey, the ascent had been quite gradual. The descent into Chile was accomplished in less than an hour on often steep and twisting roads, with 37 hairpin bends to cope with: a good way to test the brakes, which did their job very well.

On arrival in Chile, the group was met by Daniel Elton-Heavy, whose family had hosted John Coleman on his crossing. A distance of 1350 miles was covered from the Argentinian border to Northern Chile, and they passed through several desert regions, including the Atacama, reputed to be the driest place on earth. It was here that Jack experienced the first of several issues: a blown head gasket that required changing, and had to be done a second time when it failed at Iquique. On this occasion Jack was able to get the cylinder head skimmed before re-assembling it.

Diana and River were experiencing problems with the gearbox on their Chummy, whilst Stan had to replace the propshaft's fabric coupling, and also repair a leak in the radiator of his car.

The group reached Arica on the border of Peru on 8th March, then crossed into Tacna, where the Chummy misbehaved with minor electrical problems that were resolved overnight.

Approaching Arequipa a few days later, they were stopped at the roadside by one Rafael Lucioni, who had heard

South America's highest mountain, Aconcaqua, on the border of Argentina and Chile (taken 26th February 2013).

of their journey and was on the lookout for them. The cars were left with Rafael while the group visited the Colca Canyon, which, in places, is twice the depth of the Grand Canyon in America.

Resuming their journey a few days later, Jack's car fell ill, and had to be transported to a garage in Lima, while they continued their journey with the two remaining cars. On arrival in Lima on 18th March, they made their way to the garage where Jack's car had been transported, and decided to carry out some work on all three Sevens before continuing their journey.

Bertie needed to have its engine stripped down in order to try and find the cause of the low compression that necessitated the garage visit; Feisty's gearbox was making strange noises, whilst Dusty needed work on the propshaft coupling. The cause of the low compression was found to be due to broken piston rings; the gearbox problem was due to the main shaft being able to move forwards. Fortunately, the garage owner was able to locate replacement piston rings, whilst River flew home and brought back a replacement gearbox as hand luggage. Very soon all of the faults had been rectified and they were back on the road once more.

The group left Lima on 26th March, very grateful to Javier, the garage owner,

In Northern Chile on part of the original Pan-American Highway (over which John Colman had driven), 7th March 2013.

A roadside repair.

without whose help they would have been in real trouble. Their route now took them along the Pacific coast with its majestic landscape, which they found most enjoyable, and then across into Ecuador on 31st March (Easter Sunday).

It was here that John Coleman had been unable to continue his journey north due to a landslip, and from where he had boarded a boat to take him from Guayaquil to Panama. The group was able to take the road through Cuenca to Quito; climbing all the while towards Volcano alley, the Equator, and the highest point at 12,000ft above sea level.

The 85 octane petrol – all they were able to get – made the climb a very slow one. Diane and River's Chummy, in particular, was forced to tackle some of the climbs in reverse, and without a passenger. At that height they were often driving above the clouds, where it was cold and misty.

On 7th April they crossed into Columbia, where they were asked to wait at a petrol station whilst the owner called her car-mad brother who, having heard about their journey, was soon on his way to meet them. He and his wife took them to a hotel, where a good discount was arranged, and also introduced them to various people who lived along the route to Cartagena, their final leg in South America. The day after leaving the hotel an oil pipe broke on Bertie, but parts were soon found, enabling them to continue on their way.

By 14th April, after travelling 5783 miles, they had reached the Spanish colonial city of Cartagena: the humidity there, as they dropped down towards sea level, making itself felt. Now they needed to arrange for their cars to be shipped to Panama, where, before continuing their journey, the three Austins would each be given a complete service.

What should have been a two-day journey took ten, due to a breakdown of the ship transporting the cars. The port of Colon was finally reached on 30th April, and,when off-loaded, a problem with the Chummy that had been brewing since Ecuador, came to a head with loss of power and excessive smoke from the exhaust.

With the engine removed, enough compression rings were found to resolve the issue, and, once satisfied it was fixed, they were able to continue their journey a couple of days later. Just as they were about to set off, however, a bolt that held the starter motor stripped, and had to be repaired.

Heading now towards the border with Costa Rica, all three Austins were running well. Upon reaching Nicaragua, a minor accident caused damage to Chummy's windscreen and hood, necessitating a repair.

On now through Honduras and into El Salvador, where they were met by members of the National Antique Car Club who had come to greet them. Guatemala was next, and they were invited to lunch with members of the Antique Car Club of Guatemala, who they had met on the road shortly before reaching the city.

Leaving Guatemala they were escorted to

A cavalcade of cars from the El Salvador Car Club, 14th May 2013.

an unexpected overnight stop in Antigua, a Spanish colonial city and World Heritage site, where they decided to stay for a couple of days to enjoy this unexpected gem.

The group had, naturally, experienced many border crossings during the course of their journey, having to adjust their watches many times in line with local time. However, the crossing into Mexico proved farcical as, on completing the paperwork, Jack's name was queried, as his V5 document was in the name of John. The officious border officer would not accept that whilst his real name was John he had always been known as Jack. The official then insisted that Jack transfer the car to his partner, whose signature and name on her passport coincided: a process that delayed them for just over three hours.

Forewarned that Mexico was a dangerous country, because they stood out, the group decided to stick to well-travelled roads and not enter Mexico City or drive after dark.

In Monterrey, they were met by members of the Monterrey Antique Car Club. As the director of the club led them into the city, they were joined by a cavalcade of classic (American) cars. On their final day in Mexico the group was escorted by club members, who came along to ensure their safety. Both police and military were visibly present also, so they did not feel too concerned.

At the border crossing they joined the hundreds of other cars eager to cross into the United States, and what the process lacked in speed was made up for in hostility. At no time were the cars examined, but the minutiae of paperwork took priority, making this one of the longest border crossings of the entire trip.

Once through, and taking the highways rather than the interstates, the group passed through sleepy backwaters of small-town America, stopping at lunchtime diners, or picknicking by the roadside. Through Texas, Louisiana, Mississippi, Alabama, South and North Carolina they motored, on their penultimate day passing through Newark then New Jersey to a house they had

Bertie posing in front of the pyramid of the sun in Teotihuacan, Mexico.

Juan Escareno at the museum of the motoring club of Monterrey, where they parked for the night.

arranged to rent, where they were able to relax and reflect on the organisation and experiences of their five-month journey.

After arranging for the three cars to be containerised and shipped to the UK, their sights were set on the final leg of their journey: the drive into New York and Times Square. Departing just as dawn was breaking in order to avoid the worst of the traffic nightmare of a New York rush hour, feeding into the New Jersey Turnpike they traversed the industrial skyline of Newark, then on through Holland Tunnel running beneath the Hudson River, and emerging on Fifth Avenue, where they turned north to arrive at Times Square at around 6:15am.

Journey's end: Times Square in New York, June 2013.
Cars (l-r):
VW 811: a 1929 Chummy called Feisty, owned by Diana Garside and River Dukes.

XJ 1877: a 1932 RN Saloon called Dusty, owned by Stan Price.

HSJ 180: a 1933 RP Saloon called Bertie, owned by Amanda Peters and Jack Peppiatt.

Not quite sure what to do next, having achieved their goal of driving three elderly Austin Seven motor cars from Buenos Aires to New York, they decided to park three abreast on a short stretch of pavement in the middle of the square. During their stay there for best part of an hour, they were neither quizzed nor hassled while the drivers made the most of the time just taking in the atmosphere and reflecting on the adventures they had experienced during their 11,262-mile adventure, travelling through 13 countries with three crossings of the Andes; making countless new acquaintances, and experiencing many acts of kindness. All made possible thanks to Lord Austin's (relatively) 'Dependable Austin' (Seven)!

Chapter 19

Agricultural Austins

I n *The Austin Advocate Magazine* of December 1917, The Austin Motor Company was certainly looking forward to when peace was once more the order of the day. The subject of the article to which I am referring is entitled 'The Plough Again,' and anticipates a time when farmland would be cultivated without the need for, or use of, horses, as the population of these powerful beasts had been considerably reduced in the service of His Majesty's Government, pulling guns instead of the plough shares for which they had been bred.

Several types of tractor were shipped from the USA during the war, and The Austin Motor Company was entrusted to test them, determining their suitability for use in British fields. For this, an initial demonstration took place on a farm belonging to a Mr Peter Reilly at Newton Hyland, near Dublin.

Various tractors of American origin undergoing suitability trials.

Tractors of various makes seen at the Austin tractor demonstration in Ireland.
Top: Interstate tractor driving farm machinery, T/L & T/R: Killen-State tractor driving a threshing machine. Middle: The Bates 'Steel Mule' seen ploughing. B/L & B/R: The Killen-State tractor ploughing, Bottom: Interstate tractor loaded onto Austin lorry on the day following the demonstration.
(Courtesy *The Austin Advocate Magazine*)

The land selected for the various trials was well suited for testing the capabilities of the tractors employed, and involved ploughing, hill-climbing and working over rough terrain.

Three types of tractor were tested: the Interstate, the Killen-State, and the Bates Steel Mule, all eminently suited to the type of work for which they were designed and manufactured, and all of which were to be sold through Austin dealerships.

The Interstate tractor was priced at £425. Powered by a 30hp Buda petrol/paraffin engine, it was capable of pulling a three-furrow plough. The clutch was hand-operated, and the two-speed and reverse drive was taken through spur gears to the 60in diameter rear wheels.

The Killen-State was supplied with either a 30 or 40hp engine, and sold at £500 and £520 respectively. Steering was via a single front wheel; it was driven by caterpillar tracks at the rear, and could haul five tons along a road.

Of the three, the Bates Steel Mule at £485 was by far the heaviest. Powered by a four-cylinder engine, it had one forward and one reverse gear, and was capable of dragging its 2½-ton weight along a road on caterpillar tracks. However, it was considered to be quite unstable, with a tendency to topple over without warning. A later modified version was found to be totally unsuitable for use on roads, as its driving wheels left deep tell-tale furrows in its wake.

All of the tractors were designed to run on paraffin once the engines had been started using petrol.

During 1917, a Mr WE Walker was employed by Austin as Sales Manager for the newly-established Tractor Department. He later left to become Sales Manager of the Vulcan Car Agency Ltd,

The Culti Tractor was adapted to run on stored gas. (Courtesy *The Austin Advocate Magazine*)

which took over the American tractor interests with Austin's blessing: Austin, by then, had decided that the tractors were totally unsuited for use in this country, and as late as 1919 was still offering them at greatly reduced prices.

Another tractor sent to the UK had been developed by Henry Ford, and designed around the engine of the Model T. Unlike most of those previously trialled in Dublin, the engine formed an integral part of the machine, doing away with the need for any kind of chassis. The Ford offering performed very well during tractor-ploughing trials, and attracted considerable attention, to the extent that, following further trials, the Government decided that a large number of these should be assembled in the UK, to be known as Fordson MOM tractors.

Henry Ford not only provided all the patents for his tractor, but also provided a number of his staff to oversee their manufacture, and at no cost. The parts were manufactured in America and assembled in Ford's Manchester factory under Ministry of Munitions (MoM) supervision. The only proviso Ford made was that the tractors would not be sold, but loaned or hired to those who needed to use them.

By now Herbert Austin had reviewed all types of tractor available, and felt confident

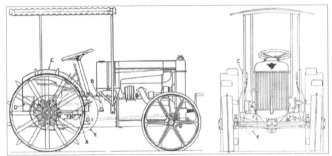

Side, front and plan
view of the first
'prototype' Austin
tractor.
(Courtesy John
Baker – *Austin
Memories*)

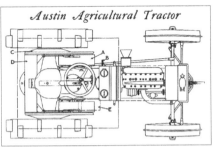

that, by incorporating all of their good features, he could design and manufacture a tractor that would be perfectly suitable for conditions in Great Britain.

The first Austin tractor, the R-type, using a modified engine from the Twenty horsepower car, was launched in 1919, and went into production in June the following year, by which time 66 machines had been manufactured. By the end of 1920, Austin had built 1500 tractors, which had sold well at between £300 and £360. The tractor at that time represented about one third of Longbridge production output.

By early 1921, Austin had effectively cornered the market, as the Fordson tractor, which was now being manufactured in the USA and imported to Britain, though selling at the same price, was subject to a 33⅓ per cent purchase tax surcharge known as the McKenna Duty. When that surcharge was later removed, Ford was able to undercut Austin by lowering the price to £120; Austin responded by slashing the price of his tractor to £225, then later down to £195.

Another company from Chicago was also importing tractors, but was certainly not welcomed by Austin. The company concerned, which specialised in earth-moving equipment, had changed its name from The Jacob Steel Excavator Company in 1917 to FC Austin Company (Incorporated), and was marketing its tractors as 'Austin Tractors' in the UK. Herbert Austin issued an injunction against FC Austin, citing that by using the name 'Austin' damage could be caused to The Austin Motor Company, and

An artist's impression of the
first Austin tractor.
(Courtesy John Baker – *Austin
Memories*)

**Early Austin R-type tractor undergoing
ploughing trials.
(Courtesy John Baker – *Austin Memories*)**

**An Austin tractor undergoing trials on
farmland owned by SF Edge in 1919.
(Courtesy John Baker – *Austin Memories*)**

**Austin tractors awaiting delivery from
Longbridge. (Author's collection)**

**A preserved tractor on display
at the Scorton Show, North
Yorkshire in 2007.
(Owner unknown)**

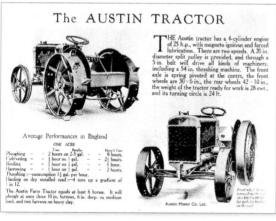

**A page from the Austin catalogue.
(Author's collection)**

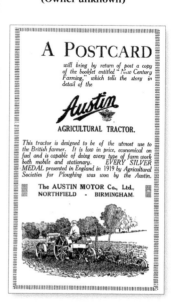

**A 1920 advertisement, described as a
'Postcard,' promotes the Austin R-type
tractor. (Courtesy John Baker)**

that, with immediate effect, it was to cease using the word 'Austin' when advertising its products.

Demand from France for agricultural machinery was at that time very strong, and Austin was, of course, keen to exploit this by selling his tractor to French farmers who considered it a very fine machine. However, the protectionist French Government decided to place very high import tariffs on all 'foreign' goods, making them very costly when these and transport costs were added to the price.

In order to get around this, Herbert Austin sought to find premises in France where the Austin tractor could be manufactured, thus avoiding the import duty and transport costs. In addition, by effectively being French-built,' he reasoned they would appeal to French patriotism.

Hence, in 1919, the Société Anonyme Austin was established, with the registered address of 139, Rue Lafayette, Paris; Sir Herbert Austin holding the majority of shares.

The factory Austin purchased was in a town called Liancourt, not that far from Paris, and was duly supplied with all of the equipment required to manufacture a French version of the Austin tractor. Once established in the August of 1919, the factory was capable of manufacturing 2000 tractors every year. To start with production was very slow, with only about 10 manufactured per month, but this figure gradually increased, leading to 80 per month within the next couple of years.

Arrangements were made for the tractors to be sold through an agent named TH Pilter, with premises in Paris.

La Maison Pilter had been involved in the sale and distribution

A postcard showing the Austin tractor factory at Liancourt, which was a former tannery.
(Courtesy John Baker – *Austin Memories*)

of tractors since 1911, commencing with the 'Ivel,' a British-made machine from Biggleswade in Bedfordshire rated at 14 horsepower and weighing 1.4 tons

This arrangement appeared to work well for a time, but in the January of 1921 Pilter suddenly refused to take any more tractors from the Liancourt factory. Why this was is not totally clear, but it is thought that the success the Fordson tractor enjoyed in France may have been a deciding factor.

The first tractor to be manufactured at Liancourt was the 'R' type, which was exactly the same as those being made at Longbridge.

Once production got under way, annual production figures gradually improved, and the design of the R-type began to take on a more 'French' appearance, with a change to the radiator design around 1923/24.

By 1923, Sir Herbert Austin had decided to concentrate all his efforts on the manufacture of motor cars, and, to this end, decided to cease production of tractors – by now manufactured to a high standard – in France. The last Longbridge tractors were sold off a year later.

By the late 1920s, the R-type was redesignated as the BO28, and this period also saw the introduction of 'Le Tracteur Vigneron,' a smaller version for use in vineyards. The 'V33' was just 95 centimetres wide and had smaller diameter front wheels.

In 1932 Austin SA launched its first diesel-engined tractors, the 16/28 and the 22/36. Production of these continued until 1940 when the factory was taken over by the invading Germans who, now under control of Krupps, used its production

A 1926 French version of the Austin R-type tractor.
(Courtesy R J Wyatt)

facilities for manufacturing war materials, although the factory did also continue to manufacture tractors until 1942.

By the late 1930s, Herbert Austin had begun to offload his shares in Austin SA, and sold most of them to Robert Rothschild, who passed them on in 1940 to his brother-in-law, Milos Celap. Shortly after that, Rothschild went with his wife to live near friends who managed the Austin tractor dealership near Lyons. Betrayed to the pro-German Vichy Government, he was arrested and sent to a concentration camp at Drancy, from which he was later transported to Auschwitz where, in March of 1944, he was murdered.

After the war, Liancourt resumed tractor production on a much smaller scale, and finally closed its doors in 1953.

Advertisement for the Austin tractor described as a BO28.
(Courtesy John Baker)

A later version of the French-built V33 tractor showing smaller front wheels. (Courtesy John Baker – *Austin memories*)

Chapter 20

The Mighty Atom

It was back in the early 1970s, whilst on a visit to Longbridge, that I was introduced to the series of promotional films that The Austin Motor Company made during the 1930s. I was shown one entitled *The Mighty Atom,* which featured the many different ways in which the Austin Seven's versatile little engine could be used, other than just for powering the family motor car.

The film showed several examples of how, with a little skill and ingenuity, these small 7hp engines could be used to power tractors, miniature railway motive power units, racing cars, speed boats, and even motorcycles.

The Austin Motor Company had commissioned several professionally produced 16mm films extolling the virtues of its products, which were distributed to main dealerships, together with the equipment upon which they could be shown to prospective customers.

The Mighty Atom commences with two racing car versions travelling at 100mph around the track at Brooklands, where straight away we can see that the Austin Seven was not a car to be messed with. This is followed by images of Austin Sevens mastering the notorious hillclimb at Shelsley Walsh. We are also shown an example of how the owner of an orchard in Dartford, Kent had a Seven rebuilt as a small tractor to enable it to negotiate the narrow walkways between his rows of trees.

The Brough Superior BS4 motorcycle also gets a viewing (see Chapter 12), as the only motorcycle to be powered by an Austin Seven engine.

The Dartford orchard owner's tractor.
(All photos in this chapter courtesy of Barry Quann, *BMC World*)

The Ransome & Rapier mobile crane used by the Great Western Railway.

The Seven engine fitted to this
Ransome & Rapier mobile crane
had no difficulty shifting the
1-ton load.

Other such unlikely vehicles included a mobile paint-spraying unit, and a Ransome & Rapier crane used by the Great Western Railway, which apparently had no difficulty lifting loads weighing up to a ton. Then we see a strange river craft called a hydro-glider built by Mr Daily of Dudley, that driven by a small propeller – powered, of course – by the Seven engine, was capable of gliding over the upper reaches of the River Severn.

However, what especially caught my eye was the Yarmouth 15in gauge Miniature Railway, which ran along a 600yd length of track adjacent to the Norfolk pleasure beach and its scenic railway.

The YMR was the brainchild of Mr Nigel Parkinson who, having built a 14in gauge railway in his garden, decided that perhaps a more viable gauge for commercial purposes would be that of 15in. He set about building a railway to this gauge beside Great Yarmouth's pleasure beach, and had an elaborate booking office and waiting room built that straddled the tracks at South Dene Station, where there were two island platforms.

The track ran down a 1:80 incline and through a 33yd tunnel, then climbed a 1:72

The hydroplane designed to be used on the upper reaches of the River Severn.

The entrance to the Great
Yarmouth Miniature Railway.

The driver checks the engine compartment ... in which lives the Austin Seven engine.

The doors are checked.   Eager passengers jostle for the best seats.

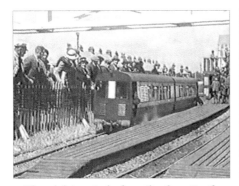 

The miniature train departing from South   The departing train, passing the adjacent
Dene Station.   scenic railway.

gradient in order for it to return to the station. Such was his attention to detail that he had the line fully signalled.

The main locomotive was originally named 'Mighty Atom,' but renamed later as the 'Prince of Wales.' The other power units were loosely based on the Metropolitan

Their journey takes them along the Great Yarmouth seafront.

Railway's 'T' Stock with the small carriages built as replicas of current main line coaches complete with corridors, The leading 'cars' were powered by ... Austin Seven engines!

The line opened in 1930 and ran for just seven years before closing in 1937.

Before leaving Longbridge I was presented with a number of stills from *The Mighty Atom*, a few of which have been included in this chapter.

This film, together with a couple of the others, have since been transferred onto VHS, and are now available as a DVD from the British Heritage Museum at Gaydon.

Chapter 21

Austin slogans

Most of us will be familiar with the Austin slogan used in the late 1920s and early 1930s: "You buy a car, but you invest in an Austin." How true that has turned out to be, as those of us who purchased one, and still have it today, will certainly appreciate the fact that their century-old Austin has risen considerably in value as the years have rolled by.

The first recorded slogan appeared in 1912: "Austin, the car that has set the fashion." Then, of course, the 1914-18 war started, bringing an end, albeit temporarily, to promoting motor cars of any make. After that we see a flurry in 1922, when, it should be remembered, the Company was in financial trouble, though still came up with "The Empire's Car," "The Sign of British Endurance," and "The Power to Purchase and Enjoy," followed a year later by another oft-remembered slogan: "Buy an Austin and banish care."

In 1931 we see a new and somewhat catchy slogan in "As Dependable as an Austin," which says a lot for the Company's faith in its products' reliability.

In 1933, seemingly not satisfied with any of these slogans, the Company ran a competition in *The Austin Magazine*, where cheques for ten shillings and sixpence (52½p) were awarded to readers who came up with a slogan showing an original or innovative style that caught the editor's eye.

Captain GA Williamson who, we are told, was a Board of Trade officer, received his cheque for: "Buy an Austin; you can bank on what you save," while Mr TH Woolley of Lapworth near Birmingham came up with: "Turn liability into reliability by buying an Austin," and Mr Alexander J Kirkbright from Stockton-on-Tees submitted: "Peace through constant revolutions."

It's very doubtful that the Company used any of these slogans in advertising campaigns, but no doubt the competition provided its participants with many hours of enjoyment, attempting to come up with something a little different from those already in use.

The editor commented that the above three examples all made good points about Austin motor cars, and showed a high degree of originality in their presentation, but they still had to go a long way to beat those actually used.

Chapter 22

And, finally ...

This chapter includes further information that has come to light regarding subjects published in the two previous volumes.

In Chapter 5 of *An Austin Anthology* (Book I), I covered the period where the McKenna Duties, introduced during the First World War to protect Great Britain from non-essential (luxury) imports such as motor cars, were rescinded in the early 1920s, and how Sir Herbert Austin got into serious trouble by challenging the Government's decision to do so.

Chancellor of the Exchequer Philip Snowden took exception to a letter written by Sir Herbert Austin, asserting how the duties had protected the British car industry, and that to do away with them would open the floodgates to cheap imports, mainly from the USA, damaging the British motor car industry, which was struggling to get back on its feet after the war.

As a result, Herbert Austin was threatened with prosecution under the Emergency Powers Act, as the Chancellor considered that Austin's letter was nothing short of blackmail. Nothing further was heard, however, and the McKenna Duties were reinstated, remaining in force until the Suez Crisis of 1956.

Shortly after the news of Snowden's climbdown had been ratified and made public, the following message was published by Sir Herbert Austin, as follows:

We have been fortunate in being able to work under the protection of the McKenna Duties, and there is no doubt that it is owing to this fact that our progress has been so consistent and rapid. Had these duties not been reinstated on July 1st 1925, The Austin Company would certainly not be in the happy position it is today. Not because we do not possess the necessary ability or courage, but because the conditions resulting from the competition of low wages on the Continent and the enormous production for home market demand in the United States would have made the task nigh on impossible. By showing that these duties have not acted unfavourably to the home purchaser, we have been able, by the confidence that these duties have given us, to reduce our selling prices by more than 65% since they were put into force, and we have also built up a considerable export trade.

We are still getting the lion's share of the British export trade: the Austin Seven is, amongst British cars, certainly the world's best seller. Since it was introduced, we have shipped more than 30,000 Baby Austins, and they can be found in practically every market in the world.

Included in Chapter 6 of *An Austin Anthology II* (The Austin Sevens that ran on rails), is a photograph of a converted Austin Seven open tourer sitting on the railway track in front of one to the South African Railway's largest and most powerful locomotives. On a recent visit to the Buckinghamshire Railway Centre, I was greatly surprised to see an example of this type of locomotive awaiting restoration.

South African Railways 4.8.4. Class 26 steam locomotive, now awaiting restoration at the Buckinghamshire Railway Centre. (Author's collection)

A similar locomotive (without smoke deflectors) with a diminutive Austin Seven converted for railway use by Permanent Way staff back in 1932. (Author's collection)

The image right depicts a full-page advertisement extolling the virtues of the new Austin 20/4 that had recently competed in the 1914 Austrian Alpine Trials.

The story of this event, and how the Austin (the only British car entered) had performed, is covered in *An Austin Anthology II.*

It's interesting to note that the event took place not long before the outbreak of war, and although it was won by a German in a Mercedes, the German motoring press, now a few months into the war, had a field day pulling apart the statements in the advert, and those appearing in the British motoring press at the time.

The full page advertisement extolling the virtues of the Austin 20. (Courtesy Rev John Campbell)

CONQUEROR OF THE ALPS !

(Under observation of the whole motoring world — official and otherwise.)

Magnificent Performance

of the *Austin* 20 h.p.

IN THE GREAT AUSTRIAN ALPINE TRIALS

Only one Austin Car entered.

COMPLETING THE WHOLE JOURNEY OF 1800 MILES IN EIGHT DAYS CLIMBING 107,523 FEET

with only one mechanical stop, caused by water in the petrol, due to torrential rains when replenishing.

(Subject to Official Confirmation).

The Austin also made

FASTEST TIME ON FORMULA

in the Katschberg Hill Climb, and at Vienna in the Speed Trial made THIRD FASTEST TIME OF ALL CARS, viz.,

63 MILES PER HOUR.

No seals were broken, and at the final examination the car was passed as perfect, in spite of the terrible conditions of the Trials.

THE AUSTIN MOTOR CO. (1914), LTD.
LONGBRIDGE WORKS, NORTHFIELD, BIRMINGHAM.

London : 479 to 483, Oxford Street (near Marble Arch), W. Depots at Paris, Manchester, and Norwich. Sub-Depots at Exeter, Oxford and Tonbridge Wells.

Agents in Russia :
BALTIC TRADING CO.
St. Petersburg.

Finally, in Chapter 18 of Book II (The 100hp Austins,) the fate of the four cars especially modified to compete in the 1908 French Grand Prix were traced as far as could be determined. The three Austin competitors in the 1908 French Grand Prix held on the streets of Dieppe were: John Brabazon, Warwick Wright, and Dario Resta. All three 100hp cars came to grief, including the spare driven by Resta.

The photo below is of Resta's car after having been completely rebuilt. Jack Johnston (the boxer) wanted to purchase one, and noted Resta's car was for sale: on hearing of the car's history, however, he thought better of it, and approached Austin to make him a new one, which he did, but with a 60hp engine.

While we can accurately trace what happened to the genuine racers, the fate of Jack Johnson's car has never been followed up. However, in a small advert published in the May 1914 edition of *The Autocar*, spotted by reader David Howe, there appears the following: "100hp Austin 1912, 2-seat racer: any car taken in exchange – George Newman and Co, 307, Euston Road. Phone: Regent 5571."

Whilst there is no evidence that this was Jack Johnson's Austin, the fact that it was dated as 1912 would certainly lead one to assume that it probably was.

Dario Resta's car now completely rebuilt, but Johnston decided against purchasing it.
(Courtesy Mr David Howe)

More great Austin books:

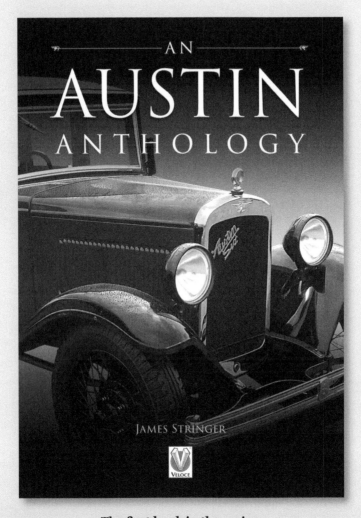

The first book in the series.
An engaging collection of short stories featuring some of the more unusual
products that came out of Longbridge, such as the 40hp motor car,
probably the first motor home ever built, and the bi-plane small enough to
keep in a garage.

ISBN: 978-1-787111-91-2
Hardback • 21x14.8cm • 112 pages • 109 b&w pictures

For more information and price details, visit our website at
www.veloce.co.uk • email: info@veloce.co.uk • Tel: +44(0)1305 260068

More great Austin books:

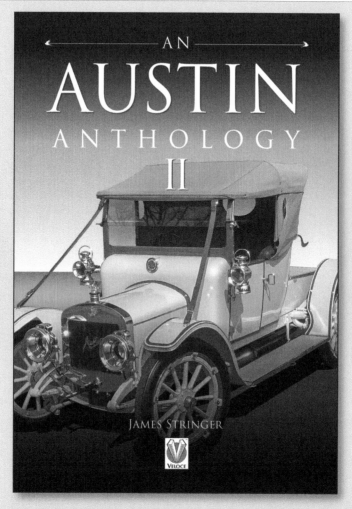

Following on from Jim Stringer's first *Austin Anthology*, this second volume unearths some more delightful vintage Austin stories, with original period photos, making this an amusing and pleasurable read for all Austin enthusiasts. Find out about the Austin Seven that ran on rails; what Hitler asked when he visited the Austin stand at the Berlin Motor Show, and the mystery of two garages – 217 miles apart, but sharing the same photograph.

ISBN: 978-1-787114-26-5
Hardback • 21x14.8cm • 112 pages • 154 colour and b&w pictures

For more information and price details, visit our website at
www.veloce.co.uk • email: info@veloce.co.uk • Tel: +44(0)1305 260068

Those were the days ... ™

VELOCE

The Last Real
Austins

1946 to 1959

HB 7049

The Last Real Austins examines how Austin bounced back after WWII, and
how, despite the severe materials shortage, it developed the largest range
of vehicles produced by any automaker in postwar Britain. It reveals how
these vehicles were received and used, and is illustrated with rare archive
photography. This book is from Veloce's popular 'Those Were the Days'
series: see our website for more nostalgic titles in this series.

ISBN: 978-1-787111-12-7
Paperback • 19x20.5cm • 96 pages • 89 colour and b&w pictures

For more information and price details, visit our website at
www.veloce.co.uk • email: info@veloce.co.uk • Tel: +44(0)1305 260068

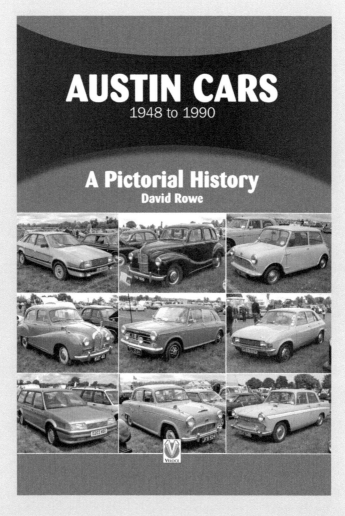

AUSTIN CARS
1948 to 1990

A Pictorial History
David Rowe

A full-colour comprehensive guide to all Austin cars built from 1948 until the end of production in the 1990s, with an informative history, detailed model-by-model comparisons, and technical information.

ISBN: 978-1-787112-19-3
Paperback • 21x14.8cm • 112 pages • 275 colour and b&w pictures

For more information and price details, visit our website at www.veloce.co.uk • email: info@veloce.co.uk • Tel: +44(0)1305 260068

INDEX

www.veloce.co.uk
Details of all current books • New book news • Special offers